CSI:

CRIME SCENE INVESTIGATION

THE INSIDER'S GUIDE TO THE TV PHENOMENON

CSI:
CRIME SCENE INVESTIGATION

THE INSIDER'S GUIDE TO THE TV PHENOMENON

ISBN 9781848566033

Published by
Titan Books
A division of
Titan Publishing Group Ltd
144 Southwark Street
London
SE1 0UP

First edition April 2010
10 9 8 7 6 5 4 3 2 1

Visit our website:
www.titanbooks.com

ACKNOWLEDGEMENTS
Titan Books would like to thank the cast and crew of *CSI*, past and present, who gave up their valuable time for the interviews included in this book, and in particular our thanks to Executive Producer Carol Mendelsohn for the Foreword. Thanks also to Veronica Hart, Maryann C. Martin, Megan Pieper and Suzanne Reed at CBS. And for their contributions to this book thanks must go to Jen Anstruther (pp41-43), Bryan Cairns (pp20-21, 26-29, 44-45, 52-57, 76-80, 88-93, 114-119, 146-151, 160-163, 164-167), Zoe Hedges (pp8-11), Sarah Herman (pp84-85, 120-121), Emma Matthews (pp8-11, 18-19, 72-73, 81-83, 106-107, 142-143), Emma Morgan (pp30-33, 46-49), Carly Roberts (pp174-175), Hannah Tibbetts (pp22-25, 108-111, 154-157), James White (pp58-59, 62-67, 94-98, 138-141, 152-153), and to Kate Lloyd (pp8-11, 12-17, 36-40, 62-67, 132-137).

A CIP catalogue record for this title is available from the British Library.

Printed and bound in China.

CSI:

CRIME SCENE INVESTIGATION

THE INSIDER'S GUIDE TO THE TV PHENOMENON

TITAN BOOKS

CONTENTS

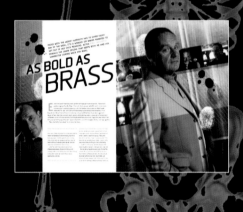

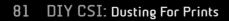

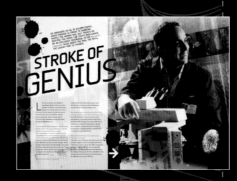

FOREWORD

From the beginning, *CSI* has been the place that crazy killers call home: Paul Millander; the Blue Paint Killer; the Miniature Killer; the Alien Lizard Killers; the Killer Ground Squirrels; and this season's Dr Jekyll. It's also been the place where the audience has been invited to go where they've never gone before: Lady Heather's Domain; a Plushies and Furries Convention; a Little People's Convention; Cirque du Soleil; Harry's Hog Hideout. And so many more. And throughout, there have been those moments that have brought us all to tears: the death of Warrick; the assassination of Sam Braun; Grissom's departure: and the abduction, rescue, departure and then return of Sarah Sidle.

As I look back over the last ten years – I'm reminded of our humble beginnings. *CSI* was a small show with a big idea: How do real crime scene investigators solve crimes? It turned out this was a question the world wanted an answer to as well.

After over two hundred episodes, my recall of cases is not exhaustive. But I recall every single episode of Season One, in detail, as if it were yesterday. Anthony, Ann and I flew by the seat of our collective pants, got an overnight degree in forensic science, and little sleep as we struggled to put science on the page and on the screen. Before long, DNA swabs, blood spatter patterns and ridges and whorls were being discussed at dinner tables around the world. Together, we all became CSIs.

First came *CSI*, then *CSI: Miami* and *CSI: New York*. The three series did more than show something that hadn't been seen before on TV, they created a new genre – the crime procedural. And the creation of our ground-breaking

series is what fills these pages.

This book captures the life of the shows. Immortalizes the efforts of hundreds of people who have contributed their talents: the crews; actors; writers; directors; editors; casting directors; special effects artists; designers; producers and the real-life CSIs who keep us real and have helped us every step of the way.

For every adventure our CSIs have had on screen, those of us behind the camera have had one ourselves in telling the story. Now, you will have the chance to go behind the scenes and hear our stories. This is our diary, capturing the intimate moments of what it was like to make the shows.

Welcome to the world of *CSI*.

Carol Mendelsohn
Executive Producer/Showrunner

10

THINGS YOU DIDN'T KNOW ABOUT LAS VEGAS...

THE LAS VEGAS WE SEE ON *CSI: CRIME SCENE INVESTIGATION* IS A FAST AND FURIOUS METROPOLIS. IT'S A CITY THAT, WITH ITS BRIGHT NEON LIGHTS, 24-HOUR CASINOS AND SPRAWLING HOTELS, NEVER, EVER SLEEPS. BUT HOW ACCURATE IS THIS DEPICTION? USING EXAMPLES FROM THE SHOW, WE REVEAL THE REALITY OF LIFE IN 'SIN CITY'...

LAS VEGAS HAS SOME OF THE HIGHEST CRIME RATES IN THE US!

Las Vegas has been dubbed "organized crime's promised land" and with good reason – the city was built largely on funding from mobsters after World War II. Today, Las Vegas, with a population of just over half a million, has some of the highest crime rates in the US, with car theft double the national average. Robbery and murder also rate highly compared with the rest of America.

On the show: Las Vegas' crime statistics are the reason *CSI: Crime Scene Investigation* creator Anthony E. Zuiker chose to set the series in the city – the Vegas crime lab is the second most active in America, after the FBI lab at Quantico, Virginia.

THERE ARE MORE THAN 200,000 SLOT MACHINES IN VEGAS

Las Vegas is easily the best-known gambling destination in the world, attracting 2.4 million visitors each month. These would-be millionaires have no end of options as to where to splash their cash, with nearly 90 casinos touting for their business. Games on offer include Roulette, Craps, Keno and Poker, with Keno providing the best win percentage at 27.63 per cent. Gamblers can also try their luck on the ubiquitous slot machines – in 1999, there were 205,726 slot machines in Nevada, one for every 10 residents.

On the show: Gambling has always played a key role in *CSI: Crime Scene Investigation*. In *CSI's Pilot*, Warrick leaves rookie investigator Holly Gribbs alone at a crime scene in order to place a bet, very nearly losing his job when she's shot and killed. The only reason he doesn't is because Grissom is reluctant to let one mistake ruin a life.

THE FIRST SUPER CASINO OPENED IN 1946

Jewish mobster Bugsy Siegel is often credited as the man behind the explosion of development in the Nevada desert in the 1930s. A member of the East Coast Mafia, he was sent to California in 1937 to set up gambling syndicates in the local area. Siegel though envisioned a sprawling casino in the desert, and set about making that vision a reality. Spurred on by the recent legalization of gambling in Nevada, and backed by the East Coast Mob, Siegel's casino, The Flamingo, opened to the public in 1946. The historic building survives to this day. Sadly, Bugsy didn't survive quite so long – he was murdered less than six months after his dream became a reality. These days, Vegas is better known for its shotgun weddings than its shotgun murders...

On the show: In the season seven episode *Living Legend* the team investigate the disappearance of fictional Mob boss Mickey Dunn, who vanished one night in 1977 and was never seen again. Mickey is played by rocker Roger Daltrey. Daltrey's band *The Who* sing *CSI's* theme tune *Who Are You?*

THE 'STRIP' WAS NAMED BY A COP FROM LOS ANGELES

Situated in the heart of the city, the Las Vegas Strip is a 6.7km section of Las Vegas Boulevard South, on which some of the world's most opulent casinos and hotels are located. Allegedly named by L.A. cop Guy McAfee, after his hometown's Sunset Strip, The Strip features the towering Stratosphere at its most northern point, with Mandalay Bay at the southern tip. In between lies the magnificent Bellagio with its dancing fountains. Further along the strip is the Luxor, modelled after an Egyptian pyramid, complete with a spectacular recreation of the Great Sphinx. Finally, New York-New York recreates the Big Apple in spectacular style, even boasting a 150ft Statue Of Liberty and a 203ft high rollercoaster which reaches speeds of 108km/h.

On the show: Rollercoaster fan Gil Grissom can be seen riding New York-New York's rollercoaster, known as the Manhattan Express, in season one's *Friends & Lovers*.

LAS VEGAS IS HOME TO THE WORLD'S LARGEST MECHANICAL SIGN

Las Vegas has many claims to fame, not least the giant cowboy that towers above Fremont Street, in the downtown area. At 40 feet high, 'Vegas Vic' is the largest mechanical sign in the world. Constructed in 1951, this jolly rancher used to wave his arm and say "howdy pardner" every 15 minutes, until Vegas regular Lee Marvin complained about the noise. Or so the legend goes...

On the show: In the season six episode *Kiss-Kiss, Bye-Bye*, the last shot of the episode shows old black and white footage of Vegas Vic in action.

VEGAS HAS AN ELVIS MUSEUM

Vegas' most famous resident of recent times was undoubtedly Elvis Presley, whose string of shows came to define the Vegas of the 1970s. In the 10 years Elvis played in Vegas he performed 669 shows, all to rave reviews and record crowds. He played the last of these historic gigs on December 12, 1976, just eight months before his untimely death. These days, it's impossible to walk through the streets of Vegas without spotting an Elvis impersonator, with literally hundreds of wannabe 'King's' making their living this way. There's even an Elvis memorabilia museum (Elvis-A-Rama) for the real obsessives, not to mention a rather portly-looking waxwork of the great man at Madame Tussauds Las Vegas.

On the show: Elvis, or rather Elvis impersonators, have popped up on several occasions in *CSI*, most notably in the episode *Viva Las Vegas*, where *Third Rock From The Sun*'s French Stewart dons The King's blue suede shoes.

TEMPERATURES CAN HIT 134°F

Although best known for its super casinos, Las Vegas has more to offer than just 24-hour gambling. In fact, the surrounding area boasts some of the most beautiful landscapes in the world. The Grand Canyon (one of the world's foremost tourist attractions) is a few hours drive away, while Death Valley, Red Rock Canyon and the Hoover Dam are all close by. For the trivia lovers among you, The Grand Canyon is 18 miles wide in places, almost a mile deep and dates back six million years. Death Valley, meanwhile, is one of the hottest places on Earth with temperatures regularly topping 104°F. The highest temperature ever recorded in this area was a mind-melting 134°F. The Valley also receives minimal rain, with just two inches annually.

On the show: The season four episode *Feeling The Heat* takes place during one such Vegas heatwave. After finding a baby dead in a car, Brass comments that while it's 108°F outside, it's 145°F inside the vehicle.

AREA 51 IS CLOSE BY

Area 51 is located in Nevada, about 90 miles north of Vegas. This remote piece of land is owned by the United States Department of Defense and has been the subject of many UFO conspiracy theories over the years.

On the show: In the season five episode *Viva Las Vegas* a dead alien turns up in Doc Robbins' autopsy suite. It transpires that the 'alien' is actually a minister at an alien-themed wedding chapel.

THERE ARE MORE THAN 35 WEDDING CHAPELS IN LAS VEGAS

With so many wedding chapels to choose from, Las Vegas has seen more celebrity couples tie the knot than any other city in the world. Elvis and Priscilla said their 'I do's' here, as did Richard Gere and Cindy Crawford, Bob Geldof and Paula Yates, Zsa Zsa Garbor and George Sanders and Dudley Moore and Brogan Lane.

On the show: As of the second episode of season eight, there are no married CSIs on the graveyard shift, with Catherine and Warrick both suffering messy divorces. Obviously the unsociable hours don't mix well with long-term commitment.

THERE ARE MORE HOTEL ROOMS IN VEGAS THAN ANYWHERE ELSE IN THE WORLD

It would take 288 years for one person to spend one night in every hotel room in Las Vegas – that's how many we're talking about...

On the show: In the season one episode *Cool Change* the lucky winner of a $40 million jackpot is upgraded to the Hotel Monaco's presidential suite, only to be found splattered on the pavement several hours later.

Fr
62.5kHz

I8
2.5sp

1 NEX

278

L010033
L010034
L01.35
L010036
L010037
L010038
L010039
L01.4
L010041
L010042
L010043
L010044
L01.45
L010047
L010048

WHERE THERE'S A WILL

FOR THE BEST PART OF A DECADE, WILLIAM L. PETERSEN HAS FOUGHT THE GOOD FIGHT AS *CSI: CRIME SCENE INVESTIGATION*'S ECCENTRIC UNIT CHIEF GIL GRISSOM. DEEP IN THE MIDDLE OF FILMING SEASON EIGHT, PETERSEN TAKES TIME OUT OF HIS BUSY SCHEDULE TO TALK SCIENCE, SARA SIDLE AND THE SHOW'S UNPRECEDENTED SUCCESS.

→

Beam of light: Grissom surveys
the scene in the season six
episode *Spellbound*.

WHO ARE YOU?

GIL GRISSOM PROFILE

A man as mysterious as the cases he investigates, night-shift supervisor Gil Grissom revealed little about his private life until *Still Life* (6.10), when he tells Catherine he was in the room when his father, a botany teacher, died. Gil was only nine but his father had instilled a love of insects in his son – now he had a fascination with death as well. He's a CSI "because the dead can't speak for themselves".

In *Revenge Is Best Served Cold* (3.01), Grissom tells Warrick that, by reading faces, he made enough money at poker to finance his own body farm at college. A man of science who follows the evidence, Gil believes in God but not religion. He keeps his deaf mother's rosary beads in his desk drawer – her otosclerosis threatened his hearing until an operation in *Inside The Box* (3.23) – and he can sign and read lips.

Authoritative but rarely angry, Grissom manages his team with a paternal firmness – so much so that his tentative relationship with Sara took six seasons to get going and even then remained a secret from their co-workers until Grissom was forced to reveal it, in *Living Doll* (7.24). Flirtations with anthropologist Teri Miller and dominatrix Lady Heather haven't developed into more but Lady Heather remains one of his few confidantes. In the main, Gil takes great pleasure in his work, even choosing to decorate his office with forensic anomalies (a two-headed scorpion, a fetal pig, the Miniature Killer's models). The sabbatical he took to teach in Massachusetts reaffirmed his love of his job. When he returned, he admitted, "I missed Las Vegas" – and in the season finale he said he considers Sara to be "the only person he ever loved".

> "As actors, we didn't want to play cops chasing down criminals, we wanted to play characters who out-thought other characters."

Eight years after its auspicious debut, William L. Petersen still can't quite comprehend the success of *CSI: Crime Scene Investigation*. "We always knew there were a group of people out there who would like the show if we did it the right way," he says with a chuckle. "We just didn't know the group of people would become so large."

Large is one word for it. Unprecedented is another. Recent statistics show that two billion people in 200 different countries regularly watch *CSI*. Not bad for a series that Petersen, who has played CSI unit chief Gil Grissom since the show's inaugural episode, sums up as: "taking nerds and giving them an hour's worth of primetime".

For the 54-year-old actor, there is no one secret to *CSI*'s overwhelming success. "I think there are a few things," he ponders. "Obviously, the first thing is the science. At the time, forensic science was being talked about throughout the world, but nobody really understood what it was and, in some cases, there was a lot of bad science happening. What our show provided was an opportunity to see the merits of forensic science."

And the second reason?

"People want to be entertained by television, but if possible they want to learn stuff too," Petersen continues. "So right at the beginning that was the premise – a show where people can learn things, but that was written in such a fun way, they have fun learning them. As actors, we didn't want to play cops chasing criminals down with cars, we wanted to play characters who out-thought other characters. It's fun to spend an hour with smart people!"

NIGHT OF THE HUNTER

Born in Evanston, Illinois, Petersen discovered his love of acting at Idaho State University. Following this, he ventured to Spain to study Shakespeare, before returning to his native Chicago, where he established himself as a theater actor of some note. Parts in Michael Mann's *Thief* and William Friedkin's *To Live And Die In L.A.* were next on the cards, followed by the role which would come to define his early career, that of Will Graham in 1986's *Manhunter*.

With no shortage of film offers throughout the intervening decade, a television series – even one produced by Jerry Bruckheimer – might not have seemed like the obvious choice for Petersen, but

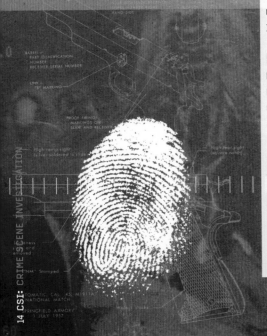

in Gil Grissom he saw a character that he could really sink his teeth into.

"In trying to decide whether to do a television show or not, my primary concern was that I didn't end up playing a character that I would get bored with right away," he explains. "I felt that any character I played would have to be someone different to me, and also someone I could care about, as opposed to a lawyer or a divorced dad or something like that. What if the show does become a hit and stays on the air? You're playing this guy every day of your life. It's got to be someone who interests you."

With his quirky outlook, insect fixation and colossal IQ, Gil Grissom is certainly interesting. According to Petersen however, the development of the character took time and teamwork. "I was allowed to participate in the creation of the character which was great," he recalls. "The idea was a smart, eccentric scientist more than anything, and he just evolved from there. The writers and I found him together and then played with it as we went along. He certainly wasn't all there when we started. It was a complete evolution of a character."

Until recently, little was known about Gil Grissom's personal life. In fact, compared with his colleagues Jim

TRUTH, JUSTICE AND THE GIL GRISSOM WAY

"Concentrate on what cannot lie. The evidence."
– *Pilot*

"God, Sara, I have so many unanswered whys."
– *Cool Change*

"I think my popsicles are ready."
– *Burden Of Proof*

"Whoa. Is that a pickle in your pocket, or are you just happy to see us?"
– *Chasing The Bus*

TRIVIA

William L. Petersen was accepted to Idaho State University on a football scholarship. But an acting class he took while at the university changed his career path.

Brass and Catherine Willows, whose turbulent private lives have been thrust into the limelight on more than one occasion, the CSI unit chief is positively a man of mystery. And that's exactly the way Petersen wanted it.

"I've never wanted there to be a lot known about the character," he elaborates. "I didn't want to be stuck with that. This way he's hard to get to know, yet interesting enough that you want to get to know him. Such as whether he was having a relationship with Sara or not, I didn't want that to be too spot on."

Ah yes, Sara Sidle. After six seasons of awkward moments, backhanded compliments and longing glances, the season six finale saw Grissom and his fellow CSI relaxing in a bedroom in their bathrobes, a scenario that confirmed a longer-standing relationship.

"We'd teased it long enough, it was time to do something about it," Petersen says simply. "I didn't want it to be what the show's about. It's like going to work and hearing too much about someone else's private life. Who cares? But I think it was time for it to happen and it was fun to let the audience in on the relationship before the other characters."

A year is a long time on *CSI* and while season six concluded on a happy note, the season seven finale was markedly different in tone, with a desperate Grissom begging miniature killer Natalie Kimble to reveal Sara's whereabouts, knowing only that she was trapped under a car somewhere in the Nevada desert.

Wary about spoiling any potential surprises for viewers, Petersen remains tight-lipped about what to expect from the coming year. He did, however,

"I'm hoping we're going to have another encounter with Lady Heather. We've been trying to keep that storyline open."

have this to say about Jorja Fox's departure, and the resulting effect it would have on Grissom...

"There are crisis points in people's lives, where the challenges they've faced and the challenges they've yet to face, force a course of action. You can find yourself changing without even knowing it and I think that's part of what's happening to Grissom this year. Things have been happening to him that he may not even be aware of and so it's a question of playing that out."

LADY IN WAITING

For all his quirks, Grissom has never been short of female attention, with Sara Sidle just one of several admirers at the Las Vegas Police Department. Then, of course, there was the beautiful and brilliant dominatrix Lady Heather, played by *The O.C.*'s Melinda Clarke.

"Melinda's a wonderful actor and we have a great chemistry," says Petersen enthusiastically. "I enjoyed working with her for the same reasons that Grissom and Lady Heather enjoyed each other. It was something completely out of the box for both of them. Grissom is a character that Lady Heather doesn't run into in her world, and vice versa. They appreciated each other in an intellectual way – I literally think they were turned on intellectually.

"Grissom loved Heather because of the way she is able to analyse people," Petersen continues. "Her ability to do this is something that Grissom is so far removed from. One of the great

TRIVIA

Petersen was offered the role of Henry Hill in Martin Scorsese's epic 1990 gangster movie, *Goodfellas* – but he turned it down. The part was ultimately played by Ray Liotta.

TRIVIA

Similar to Grissom, Petersen is an avid fan of baseball, in particular the Chicago Cubs. He even drops by Wrigley Field once a year to sing the seventh inning stretch.

mysteries of life to him is the ability to really get people and what she does better than anything else is get people on a really base level."

So will we be seeing Lady Heather again?

"I'm hoping that we're going to have another encounter with Lady Heather," confides Petersen. "We've been trying to keep that storyline open and I certainly think there's room for us to see her again."

Another *CSI* alumni that Petersen is happy to wax lyrical about is Quentin Tarantino, director of the gripping season five two-parter *Grave Danger*.

"Quentin's great," laughs Petersen. "He's incredibly skilful and brilliant, and yet he has fun like a 12-year-old at an amusement park. Sometimes he shoots for a long time, but he knows what he wants in advance and he goes out and gets it. *Grave Danger* was only supposed to be a one-hour show, but Quentin was having such a great time doing it, that it turned into two hours. We had to call the network and say, 'Listen, can we get another hour that night because our show's going to be bigger than we thought?' He just loved it!"

ALL THE WORLD'S A STAGE

Although he's spent the best part of the last decade on the small screen, William L. Petersen's first love is, and always will be, the theater. He even took some time off from *CSI* last season to do a play in his native Chicago.

"I hadn't been in a play for seven or eight years and I was worried that if it went on any longer I would be afraid to get back on the stage," he admits. "So I took some time off last Christmas and did the play, and I'm hoping to go back again next year."

Such is Petersen's passion for treading the boards that when Grissom puts away his magnifying glass for the last time, the actor will likely head straight for the Windy City. "I have a lot of friends in theaters there that I want to work with, so yes, that's pretty much what I'll probably do."

And when that time comes, what will Petersen miss most about *CSI*?

"The cast and crew," he answers emphatically. "You asked earlier about things that separate this show in some way, and we talked about the writers and the puzzles and the suspense and the forensics. One thing I didn't mention was the cast. We were able to create this cast from scratch and we really love and care about each other. For that to be the case on any show, at any time, especially after eight years, is remarkable. The cast and the crew are the thing I'll miss the most. It's a giant family." CSI

WILLIAM L. PETERSEN'S SCREEN CREDITS

A sample of Petersen's finest movie work...

Young Guns II (1990)
– as 'Pat' Garrett
In this sequel to the 1988 hit, Petersen plays Wild West lawman Patrick 'Pat' Floyd Garrett – the man responsible for killing Billy the Kid. Brat-packers Emilio Estevez, Lou Diamond Phillips and Kiefer Sutherland revive their roles from the original.

Manhunter (1986)
– as Will Graham
Directed by Michael Mann, this gripping thriller sees Petersen as an FBI agent hunting down a serial killer. Based on the Thomas Harris novel, this was the role that rocketed the *CSI* actor to fame. He's since said of the film: "After *Manhunter*, I had to actually kill off the character. I cut off most of my hair and dyed it blond. I changed my whole look just to get rid of him."

To Live And Die In L.A. (1985)
– as Richard Chance
Director William Friedkin gave Petersen his big break when he cast him as a fearless secret service agent in this action thriller.

Ever wanted to snoop around Gris' office? Peek in his refrigerator? Go through his desk? Well, here's your opportunity to have a poke around his apartment, and see what really makes Gil Grissom tick...

GRISSOM'S DESK

>> Unsurprisingly for an entomologist, the walls of Gris' home office are covered with his collection of insect specimens – mounted, framed, and proudly displayed. The bugs include a giant cicada, several butterflies and some nasty looking beetles. Alongside those are jars of anatomical animal specimens – a sheep's heart and brain and a preserved pig embryo. Considering Gil's penchant for the extraordinary, it's no surprise that his personal collection also includes some rather gruesome specimens. A wooden owl, art from his extensive travels, and what appears to be a furniture catalogue also compete for space on a crowded desk.

GRIS AND SARA

>> On the side of the fridge is a picture of Grissom and Sara in San Francisco, where they met for the first time. Slightly obscuring a recipe for turkey with mozzarella, this is yet more evidence that Gris and Sara are more serious than they ever let on to their colleagues. Clearly, Grissom has had this picture for a long time, and displayed it in the one place he, and only he, would see it every day – while making a cup of organic chamomile tea...

SEARCH
W A R R A N T

GRISSOM'S DESK, LEFT-HAND VIEW

This side of the desk shows Grissom's love of botany, probably passed down from his late father. Leaf specimens, a terrarium of plants, and some organic fertilizer show that this passion is clearly ongoing. Those plants include two carnivorous species as well as an extremely poisonous variety known as dumb cane. A vase full of porcupine quills and an identified skull are just some of the eclectic decorative items dotted around the space. A telescope nestles behind the desk, just out of reach – perhaps a sign of a past passion. And of course, no CSI would be at home (or anywhere else) without at least one box of rubber gloves! This is the neatest, most well-kept corner of the office, a quiet corner in a turbulent existence...

GRISSOM'S SHELVES

Clearly widely read, Grissom's well-stocked library consists of every subject under the sun, including criminology texts, home veterinary help, and natural history. Perhaps surprisingly for a man who deals only in evidence, his collection also includes the titles *Mysteries Of The Unexplained* and *What You Should Know About Ghosts*. Literature is well represented – leather-bound tomes including Shakespeare's Tragedies, *Crime And Punishment* and the works of Edgar Allen Poe. To say Gris is intrigued by the darker side of humanity would be an understatement! There is one author here that is a surprise, though – Sidney Sheldon. Never let it be said that Gil Grissom doesn't have a romantic side! There are two pictures of Sara and his beloved boxer Hank, and of course, a portrait of the nightshift, in happier times. Grissom's penchant for the darker side seems to have manifested itself in his art choices as well – two abstract paintings that seem to depict the devil rest on top of the bookcase.

GRISSOM'S KITCHEN

>> A clean, utilitarian space that's effectively organized – the kitchen is as quintessentially Grissom as the pig-decorated office. The vertical tap over the sink looks like it came directly from the morgue, and along with the test-tube spice rack, is yet more evidence of his often clinical nature. There are also plenty of signs that his relationship with Sara was solidifying – two cups on the drainer and two places set on the island, ready for the next meal, speaks to the amount of time they were spending together. The fridge is plastered in pictures and postcards of rollercoasters – the only obvious sign of this particular passion. The jar of dog biscuits and bowl of food on the counter point to it being Grissom's turn to look after Hank that night, but the dog food could also be for Gris' pet cockroaches!

GENIUS & MADMAN

The Professor Moriarty to Grissom's Sherlock Holmes, criminal mastermind Paul Millander led the Vegas CSIs a merry dance during the first season of the show. In an exclusive interview, actor MATT O'TOOLE recalls the life and death of this unforgettable villain.

Serial killer Paul Millander initially appeared in the CSI pilot but did you realize he would become this recurring presence?

There was one defining moment where Billy Petersen and I were waiting for the cameras to roll as they were resetting. We were talking while playing with the props and there was this shrunken head. Millander had already defined himself as somewhat different and the character takes you over sometimes. So Billy was holding this shrunken head and I said, "No please." I took it away from him, put it back very carefully, and went, "That's my brother. I like to keep my family close by." It was just fun and Billy gives me this look and goes, "Oh, you're coming back!" We laughed about the whole thing but he's such a giving professional. He became so engrossed in the process himself that perhaps Billy realized that Millander was important too.

What made Millander such a worthy nemesis for Gil Grissom?

Millander respected Grissom and thought he was brilliant in his field. Obviously, Millander did his homework, found out who Grissom was, and rather than be an adversary, he wanted to play with him or be on his team. As Millander, I wanted Grissom to see my work and perhaps we could be friends instead of this cat and mouse situation. It could have been, "Hey, look what I can do. I haven't disappointed you on this one." I often

get to play villains and there are few bad people who really think they are bad people.

Did you enjoy all the smart banter between Millander and Grissom?

As an actor, Billy was right there with me, such a professional, and so grounded that there was nothing more important than what was happening at that time. That's gold. As Millander, I thought perhaps now I was his equal and Gil was so good at not letting me see his disgust.

Were you shocked to discover Millander was born a girl?

When I first read the script, I was going along thinking it was a great story and then I realized, "Wait! What? I was a girl?" I turned the page back to read it again. There's all this back-pedaling then to figure out who I was and who I am now. It was a surprise and a telling moment where you go, "That's why I'm having these problems!" Then, of course, you embrace it. It was done with great respect because there are people in life who travel this road.

How did his death sit with you?

I was surprised. As an actor who wants more work, I'm like, "Damn! Of course he's coming back! That's his doppelganger! He found this guy and just placed him there." Honestly, he had finally given up. Millander wasn't going to let anyone else rule his life or make choices for

him. There's no way he could have lived within those trappings. My question is if Millander did get away, which he did, why couldn't he have just fled? Even though I know he was in the tub, the viewer part of me insists he wasn't.

And there was some discussion over whether Millander was going to be in the bathtub at the end. This was my final moment for showing Grissom who I was. The choice was I'd be fully dressed for this one because the bathtub was dry. It was just symbolic of his father's own death.

And yet he murdered his mother before committing suicide...

Originally, they wanted Millander to kill his wife and child. They were so wonderful about having script meetings and we all decided Millander was not an unkind soul. There was always a reason for his actions and there was no reason to kill his wife and child. And his mother did him a lot of harm in his life. But if he killed his mother, perhaps that made it easier for me to rationalize the fact that now he has to kill himself because he was the final person that made the wrong choices. He was a purist that way and not a coward. It made sense when I reviewed it because there has to be a lot of angst, fear, and anger to take someone's life.

Where can CSI viewers catch you next?

Right now, there is a movie I just finished called Truth Never Lies. It was a small project with

"**When I first read the script, I was going along thinking it was a great story and then**

a European sense of domestic drama. I get to play a doctor, a real person, who doesn't kill anyone and doesn't get killed. I said, "Are you sure there's no death scene? Not even a gun?" I'm usually running after someone or being run after! I've even had my neck broken and been shot at by Bruce Willis. CSI

I realized, 'Wait! What? I was a girl?'" >>> **SEASON** >>> **1**

GONE BUT NOT FORGOTTEN

HE MAY HAVE LEFT LAS VEGAS, BUT GIL GRISSOM'S LEGACY LIVES ON. FOR THOSE OF YOU SUFFERING WITHDRAWAL SYMPTOMS (WHICH LET'S BE HONEST, IS ALL OF US), HERE'S A LOOK AT GRISSOM'S DEFINING MOMENTS, FROM OUR FIRST INTRODUCTION TO *THAT* KISS IN THE COSTA RICAN JUNGLE...

NUTTY PROFESSOR
Gilbert Grissom, we presume...

When? *Pilot*, season one, episode one
What? One of the first impressions we get of CSI Gil Grissom is through new girl Holly Gribbs, and what an introduction it is. Standing in his office surrounded by assorted jars of insects and strange-looking samples, Grissom's first request of Holly is a pint of blood. She obliges but is left feeling unnerved and light-headed, so Grissom offers a remedy she's even more wary of – a "snack" from one of his jars! Aside from his quirky taste in office décor, we see that Grissom is a brilliant scientist, and a much-respected leader, always available to listen and offer sound advice to his colleagues. So when Detective Jim Brass tells Holly that the Las Vegas lab is second in the US rankings, it's safe to assume that this is due to Grissom's influence.

> "Concentrate on what cannot lie – the evidence."

STOLEN MOMENTS
Do they or don't they?

When? *Lady Heather's Box*, season three, episode 15
What? Grissom is the consummate professional and little is known about his private life. But when an investigation results in a second encounter with the beautiful dominatrix Lady Heather, business turns to pleasure. Or does it? The two have a meeting of minds on an intellectual level, but we're left guessing as to whether it goes any further than that. Grissom goes to Heather for advice about the case, but says that he is there as a friend. As their conversation continues, they get closer and closer and end up just inches apart with Grissom caressing Lady Heather's face. The next thing we see is the two of them sharing a morning cup of tea, and though Lady Heather is in different clothes, Grissom is wearing the same shirt and trousers he was the previous night. So how much further did their conversation go? We'll never know for sure!

> "You can always say stop."

SOUND PROOF
Grissom faces up to his hearing difficulties...

When? *Inside The Box*, season three, episode 23
What? Grissom learns that there are some things in life he can't control when his otosclerosis becomes worse. His hearing problem becomes so apparent that even a piercing bank alarm becomes a muffled sound, and he has to lip-read to fully understand his colleagues. Despite carrying on with his shift, he realizes the problem won't go away, especially when Doc Robbins warns him that delaying treatment any longer could lead to permanent deafness. Grissom schedules surgery and goes alone as a matter of course, but is noticeably touched when Catherine arrives to offer support. However, his independence (or is that stubbornness?) is still strong enough for him to refuse a wheelchair to the operating theater!

"Thank you for being here."

HOME TRUTHS
Grissom reveals his regrets over Sara...

When? *Butterflied*, season four, episode 12
What? When a murder victim strongly resembles Sara, Grissom is unnerved and plagued by thoughts of her. He takes the case very personally, almost to the point of obsession, and doesn't leave the scene for over 15 hours. Exhausted and troubled, he finally returns to the department to question the main suspect, and during the interrogation draws poignant comparisons between the murderer and himself. In a heartfelt summary, he talks of middle-aged men being given a second lease of life by the love of a younger woman, and sadly, how he felt he couldn't take the steps to embrace it. He is left alone with his thoughts – his regrets – while Sara looks on through the one-way window.

"We wake up one day and realize that for 50 years we haven't really lived at all..."

UNITED THEY STAND
Following Nick's brush with death, Grissom demands his team back

When? *Mea Culpa/Grave Danger Pts. 1 & 2*, season five, episodes nine/24/25
What? Testifying in court, Grissom's respect for the truth forces him to speak up when he notices a discrepancy in the evidence. This leads to the case being reopened and Ecklie takes the opportunity to start an inquiry into Grissom's role as supervisor. Even though the quality control officer clears Grissom of any breach of protocol, Ecklie splits the team up due to Gris' alleged "shortcomings as supervisor." Nick and Warrick are angered by the news, but with his stoic diplomacy, Grissom tries to calm them down and make the best of the situation. However, some time later, when both day and night shifts work overtime in a traumatizing effort to save Nick's life, Grissom decides that the bond his team has is too strong to break, and demands they are reunited.

"I want my guys back."

PILLOW TALK
At long last...

When? *Way To Go*, season six, episode 24
What? When Detective Brass is shot and left in a critical condition, Grissom has to use the power of attorney entrusted to him to authorize a risky operation. It's a trying time while he and the team await news of Brass' recovery, but thankfully the operation is a complete success. Later, in the privacy of his bedroom, a somber Grissom talks aloud about the day's events and his thoughts on death. It's only when Sara Sidle walks out of the bathroom that we realize he's talking to her. Dressed only in a bathrobe, it's confirmation that the relationship we'd all wished for is a reality, and looks like it has been for some time.

"I'd prefer to know in advance that I was going to die... have some time to prepare... at least have enough time to say goodbye to the people I love."

BEE MINE
Grissom pops the question...

When? *The Case Of The Cross-Dressing Carp*, season eight, episode four
What? After a rocky road to romance, Grissom decides the time has come to propose to Sara. It seems spontaneous at the time, but as Grissom's not one to enter into things lightly, he must have realized long before that he didn't want to be without Sara, and marriage would be the logical conclusion. Or perhaps the thought did suddenly occur to him – who knows what goes on in that brilliant brain of his? Luckily, Sara isn't a high-maintenance girl, so the fact that he has no ring and that the proposal comes out of the blue (while they're tending bees) is not an issue. To both his delight and ours, she happily accepts!

"You know, maybe we should get married."

ONE OF OUR OWN
Grissom is left devastated when Warrick is murdered...

When? *For Warrick*, season nine, episode one
What? After everything Grissom's been through with his team, he sees them as more than just colleagues, especially Warrick, who he regards as a son. So when he finds the Vegas-born CSI shot and left for dead, it's heartbreaking that he can do nothing but hold him in his arms as he bleeds to death. The tragic loss brings Sara back to Vegas, and it is with her that Grissom expresses how much Warrick meant to him and describes the agonizing moments in which he passed away. When a recording is discovered of Warrick paying tribute to his father figure, it's obvious that Grissom is the man he meant. Grissom's final paternal responsibility comes when he gives a touching eulogy at Warrick's funeral. With bittersweet pride, he conveys how close his team were and how much he will miss Warrick.

"Just before he died, we were all having breakfast together. Our team, his friends, his family... I'm going to miss him so much."

LOVE'S LABOR'S LOST
Grissom races against time to save Sara

When? *Living Doll*, season seven, episode 24
What? When the serial "Miniature Killer" strikes again, Grissom and the team finally apprehend her. But not before she sets up one more attack – the kidnap and attempted murder of Sara. Grissom realizes it's not just a random attack on Sara, and that the killer is targeting him in revenge for losing her foster father. With Sara's life hanging in the balance, there's no time for personal secrets, and the news of his relationship with Sara is revealed when Grissom announces his theory to the team. He questions The Miniature Killer by flattering her skill, but when this doesn't work, he loses his cool and is left desperately searching for clues and his beloved Sara.

"I took away the only thing she ever loved, so she's going to do the same to me."

TIME'S UP
Grissom bids farewell to the LVPD...

When? *One To Go*, season nine, episode 10
What? Throughout his career, Grissom has always managed to distance himself from his cases – it's one of the reasons he's such a superb CSI. But his relationship with Sara and the loss of Warrick has taken its toll, and throughout season nine we've witnessed a heartbreaking decline in his passion for his work. He seems to have lost his way as he's lost pieces of himself. So when he announces that he's leaving the team, it's no real surprise and clearly the right decision. He works his final case and takes every opportunity to talk to his team on an individual basis, offering them a sense of consolation and reassurance. These personal moments are all he has in way of a farewell, and he leaves the lab discreetly. The next thing we see is Grissom trekking through the Costa Rican jungle and we're certain that every single fan is wishing the same thing – that he finds what he's set out for, the only certain thing in his life, Sara Sidle. Pass the tissues, please...

"It's the right time for me to go."

THE TIES THAT BIND

IMPOSSIBLE TO PIGEONHOLE, LADY HEATHER HAS BEEN A SOURCE OF FASCINATION TO *CSI* FANS EVER SINCE SHE FIRST APPEARED IN *SLAVES OF LAS VEGAS*. HERE ACTRESS MELINDA CLARKE CHATS ABOUT BEING GRISSOM'S OTHER WOMAN...

What intrigued you about Lady Heather?
First of all, I don't think people understand that when you audition for a guest role you get the material the night before, around 7pm. And then you walk in around 10am – there really isn't much time to do any research. Luckily, this character was so well-conceived and written by Jerry Stahl that everything Lady Heather embodied was on the page. For me, the character fit like a glove. When you describe her as a dominatrix there are some raised eyebrows, yet it was so little about that. It was more about her being mysterious, enigmatic and intelligent – she was also so comfortable being a woman. She owns her sexuality. It was a fantasy to play a woman like that.

Were you a fan of *CSI* before taking the role?
Actually, when I got involved it was 2001 and the beginning of the second season. The year before I had read the pilot and it was my favorite for the season. I predicted it would be a hit so [its success] is because of me. [Laughs] I originally auditioned for Marg Helgenberger's role, so I was very aware of *CSI*.

Did you have to do any special preparation for such an intriguing character?
Honestly, no. For the first episode they had a dominatrix named Julianna on set. I remember asking her if she had any advice for me and she said, "No, you're a natural!" [Laughs] When the material is written well, there really isn't need for research.

At what point did you become aware of Lady Heather's popularity with *CSI* fans?
I may have been aware early on thanks to the ratings, but I didn't realize there was fan discussion. I am friends with a lot of people on *CSI*, so I would get little titbits here and there. It was just wonderful to hear the character was popular. Lady Heather is a wonderful partner to Grissom in terms of their intellect, so I can understand how viewers caught on to that.

Grissom has always seemed genuinely fascinated with Lady Heather, but what does she get out of their relationship?
I was discussing this with [executive producer] Carol Mendelsohn and how their relationship could have gone

LADY HEATHER EPISODES

Of Inhuman Bondage (9.05)
The Good, The Bad, And
The Dominatrix (7.23)
Pirates Of The Third Reich (6.15)
Lady Heather's Box (3.15)
Slaves Of Las Vegas (2.08)

Melinda Clarke
as she appeared
in The O.C.

>>>>>>> NO ENTRY POLICE LINE DO NOT CROSS NO ENTRY

Main image © Warner Bros. Television

a different way. They could have been much more intimate but they got more out of each other intellectually than physically. They were equals intellectually so most of their energy was put there.

There's a lot of debate as to whether Grissom and Lady Heather got together in season three's *Lady Heather's Box*. Care to weigh in?
Personally, when we were filming that episode, I thought they did, but Billy [Petersen] will tell you they never have. That is the official answer. He does

"You would never catch Lady Heather in flip-flops, or tennis shoes!"

← "Quotation"

spend the night, but that isn't totally clear. [You only know] because my clothes change, his don't, and they're having tea the next morning. Apparently, they stayed up talking. But in *Of Inhuman Bondage*, there's definitely a lot for the audience to talk about in respect to whether it's physical. It's going to come up again.

What are your thoughts on Lady Heather's wardrobe?
As actors, we tend to work from the inside out, which is a very American way of dealing with the process. A lot of times, with British actors for instance, people work from the outside in. Hair, make-up, and clothes are all important and, in Lady Heather's case, that means a bustier, a corset, tall boots, and a skirt with a slit. It absolutely creates a physicality. You can't have Lady Heather without those clothes. I am walking around in flip-flops today – you would never catch her in those, or tennis shoes.

The first few times we see Lady Heather, she's very much in control, but that mask slips when her daughter is murdered in *Pirates Of The Third Reich*. Did you enjoy playing a more vulnerable side to her?
It's absolutely enjoyable to explore all those aspects with her. She's usually in control, but clearly went to extremes and tried to whip her daughter's killer to death and commit suicide. That is pretty rock bottom, [and shows she's] flawed like everyone else. They've taken her to such lengths on this show. Even in this last episode, I thought, "Oh no! What are they going to do to Lady Heather this time?"

Talk us through that whipping scene in *Pirates*. It looked pretty brutal...
That scene was filmed on the coldest night. It was January, in the desert, and although it's

California, it was freezing and the poor actor being whipped was half dressed. For the whip, they used the tricks of the trade. It's not a real whip, and when it crosses the body, it feels like tissue paper. The stunt coordinator taught me how to make it look like he's really being whipped with the best stroke so it looks really violent. She really was losing it.

The original ending to *The Good, The Bad, And The Dominatrix* was tweaked. What didn't work?
The original episode left the audience feeling like there wasn't totally a conclusion. I think it was Billy's idea to have Grissom show up and arrange for the introduction to my granddaughter. That left audiences feeling like Lady Heather had a little bit of redemption. Before that ending, that didn't exist. The audience was left wondering if she was going to come back from her suicide attempt. That scene provided hope, which I think Billy was interested in.

What can you tell us about the latest Lady Heather episode, *Of Inhuman Bondage*?
Grissom is having some emotional problems with Sara not being in the picture, and Warrick being dead. He is having trouble sleeping, so he visits Lady Heather under the guise that he needs help with a case. She is no longer a dominatrix, but she does do sex therapy. This is a very different kind of episode for Lady Heather. It's literally just eight scenes of Billy and me talking about the case. She tries to get through to him and to talk about his life. Ultimately she figures out that, "Everything I've told you, you could have read in a book! I think you are here for a personal reason. You are here because this isn't work. This isn't home. This is the only place that doesn't remind you of Sara." Grissom then stays. Billy and I said it was like a little play between

them, because it was a lot of dialogue – probably the most dialogue I've had [on one episode] of any TV show ever.

Where next for Lady Heather?
One of the writers was saying we need a Lady Heather spin off. She could be a profiler, because she is so good at reading people. We were teasing that Jerry Stahl should write it and we should pitch it to CBS. It would be fascinating. She could be the next crime fighter.

Looking back, did you ever imagine Lady Heather would have such a presence on *CSI*?
Anything was possible, yes. Clearly when something works, is well-conceived, the actors enjoy it, and it fits like a puzzle piece, you want to repeat it. I believe I am back [in season nine] because of Billy. Carol asked, "If Grissom was having problems, what do you think he would do?" He said, "Grissom would go to Lady Heather."

There is this undeniable synergy...
I remember when I met Billy; the chemistry [you see on screen] was there between us [in real life]. You could tell we were just enjoying the words we were saying and the characters. This is why we do what we do. It's the exuberance children have when they are using their imagination. The other day I went to work and I said to my eight-year-old, "Mommy is so happy." And she said, "Why?" I was like, "I get to work with William Petersen and be Lady Heather again." I did have that feeling of a child going to work. It's one of my favorite jobs of all time, and Billy is a big part of that. Back in 2001, something magical happened. CSI

CASE FILE

Classic *CSI* episodes revisited!

LADY HEATHER'S BOX

EPISODE 3.15

EPISODE:
Lady Heather's Box (3.15)

FIRST SHOWN (US):
February 13, 2003

FIRST SHOWN (UK):
May 13, 2003

WRITTEN BY:
Carol Mendelsohn, Andrew Lipsitz, Naren Shankar, Eli Talbert, Anthony E. Zuiker, Ann Donahue, Josh Berman & Bob Harris

DIRECTED BY:
Richard J. Lewis

REGULAR CAST:
William L. Petersen (Gil Grissom)
Marg Helgenberger (Catherine Willows)
Gary Dourdan (Warrick Brown)
George Eads (Nick Stokes)
Jorja Fox (Sara Sidle)
Paul Guilfoyle (Capt. Jim Brass)
Eric Szmanda (Greg Sanders)

GUEST STARS:
Melinda Clarke (Lady Heather)
Michael Riley (Steven McCormick)
Amy Pietz (Rebecca McCormick)
Timothy Carhart (Eddie Willows)
Madison McReynolds (Lindsey Willows)
Pauley Perrette (Candeece)
Samuel Ball (Kiner)

GRISSOM

CATHERINE

LADY HEATHER

>>> SYNOPSIS

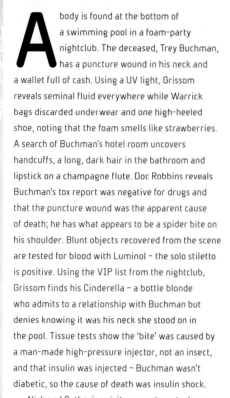

A body is found at the bottom of a swimming pool in a foam-party nightclub. The deceased, Trey Buchman, has a puncture wound in his neck and a wallet full of cash. Using a UV light, Grissom reveals seminal fluid everywhere while Warrick bags discarded underwear and one high-heeled shoe, noting that the foam smells like strawberries. A search of Buchman's hotel room uncovers handcuffs, a long, dark hair in the bathroom and lipstick on a champagne flute. Doc Robbins reveals Buchman's tox report was negative for drugs and that the puncture wound was the apparent cause of death; he has what appears to be a spider bite on his shoulder. Blunt objects recovered from the scene are tested for blood with Luminol – the solo stiletto is positive. Using the VIP list from the nightclub, Grissom finds his Cinderella – a bottle blonde who admits to a relationship with Buchman but denies knowing it was his neck she stood on in the pool. Tissue tests show the 'bite' was caused by a man-made high-pressure injector, not an insect, and that insulin was injected – Buchman wasn't diabetic, so the cause of death was insulin shock.

Nick and Catherine visit an apartment where a dead body has begun to putrefy beside a set of weight-lifting equipment. Catherine finds cash, a well-stamped passport and few possessions, leading her to believe the dead man, Croix Richards, was a drug dealer and the weight-lifting accident was staged. Daughter Lindsey calls Catherine's mobile phone in distress – she's trapped in dad Eddie's car and it's filling with water. Using local landmarks, Catherine gets Lindsey to describe where she is. Catherine finds the car in a storm drain and breaks a window to free her daughter. Lindsey tells Detective Vega a woman with pink hair was driving because Eddie had a stomach ache. Inside the recovered vehicle, Catherine finds a vial containing GHB.

Back at the lab, Doc Robbins X-rays Richards' decomposed body and sees a foreign body lodged in his femur: the tip of a needle that could be used to inject insulin. Buchman had a second hotel room, at the Tangiers – Warrick and Grissom find a woman in her underwear waiting on the bed. It becomes apparent that both Buchman and Richards were gigolos, in the employ of Lady Heather for her website, ladyheather.com. The CSIs run the credit card transactions of Buchman and Richards' local clients and find the woman from the Tangiers listed – Rebecca McCormick. Her husband, Steven, claims he hired Richards to 'dominate' his wife. Rebecca admits to also making a date with Trey, to improve her technique, but claims they had previously only interacted online.

A search of the storm drains uncovers Eddie's dead body – there's a bullet wound in his stomach. Sara processes Eddie's car and finds a demo CD that leads her to a recording studio, where the engineers recall Eddie's protégée, Candeece, throwing a fit when Eddie wasn't present for her last recording session. Sara and Vega interview Candeece; she eventually admits to seeing Eddie, who was already wounded, but when she calls Lindsey a "stupid, screaming little brat," Catherine snaps and threatens her.

Under a microscope, Rebecca McCormick's hair proves to be a match to that from Buchman's original hotel room, proving she lied about never having met him in person. Lady Heather confirms to Grissom that Rebecca's husband is a long-term client of her establishment – and an investor in her online empire – who had used her gigolos to loosen up his sexually

>>>

DOC ROBBINS   SARA   BRASS

31 CSI: CRIME SCENE INVESTIGATION

>>>

repressed wife. Grissom has early-morning tea with Lady Heather; when he offers her sugar, she reveals she's diabetic and uses a high-pressure syringe to administer her insulin injections.

Analysis of tracks recorded at the poorly-soundproofed studio the night Eddie died reveal a gunshot and engine noise outside. Candeece called biker Kiner, an ex-con on parole, from the studio – Sara finds GHB in his garage. Kiner and Candeece blame each other for Eddie's shooting.

Rebecca McCormick is murdered in her own home; Grissom finds a fragment of an ostrich feather on her body. Back at Lady Heather's

house, they examine the room of submissive Chloe Samms, who uses a feather boa as a garrotte. When Grissom finds shoes that smell of strawberry foam, Lady Heather reveals that Chloe quit yesterday and refuses to accept an apology from Grissom.

Sara is unable to prove who shot Eddie, so is only able to file lesser charges on Candeece and Kiner, leaving Catherine crushed. Greg finds Chloe's DNA on one of Lady Heather's insulin bottles – Chloe says she killed both men for Steven. He admits seeing Chloe but insists she killed Richards, Buchman and his wife on her own – the submissive was in control the whole time. CSI

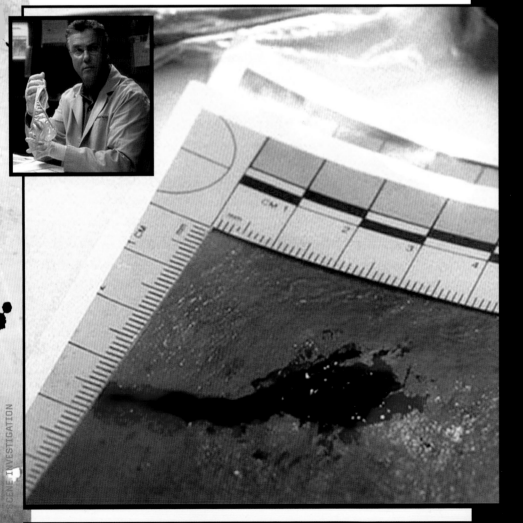

TRIVIA

NCIS star Pauley Perrette plays Candeece and sings during her flashback scenes in the studio.

Contrary to what many fans believe to have happen William L. Petersen insists that Grissom and Lady Heather did not sleep together when Grissom appea to have spent the night at her house.

Type 1 diabetics take insulin to regulate the levels of glucose in their bloodstream – without it, they could slip into a fatal diabetic coma. Excessive doses cause shock, resulting in convulsions and coma. 'Insulin shock therapy' was used in the 1950s to treat psychotic and drug-addicted patients – after an hour, patients would be given glucose or a saline solution to end their coma!

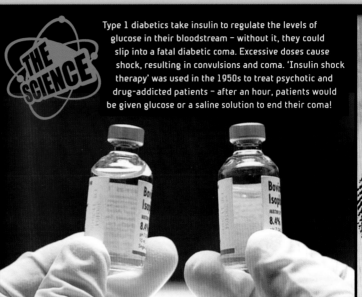

CHARACTER DEVELOPMENT: CATHERINE WILLOWS

Even before Eddie died, Catherine found raising Lindsey to be a tough task. Now totally alone, she finds it hard to rein in her emotions, flying off the handle when Candeece insults Lindsey and collapsing in tears at home when she realizes no charges will be filed for Eddie's murder. Grissom would usually come to Catherine's aid but he has personal issues of his own in this episode, getting uncharacteristically close to Lady Heather, then losing her trust when she becomes a suspect. We first met Lady Heather in *Slaves Of Las Vegas* (2.8) and she returns in *Pirates Of The Third Reich* (6.15) and *The Good, The Bad And The Dominatrix* (7.23), where her closeness with Grissom rattles Sara.

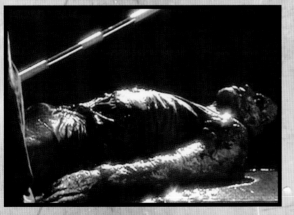

Showgirls star Elizabeth Berkeley makes a cameo as the unnamed blonde who pierced Trey Buchman's neck with the heel of her stiletto.

33 CSI: CRIME SCENE INVESTIGAT

FACED WITH THE WORST HUMANITY HAS TO OFFER EVERY DAY OF THE WEEK, IT'S A WONDER JIM BRASS MANAGES TO GET OUT OF BED EACH MORNING. ACTOR PAUL GUILFOYLE REVEALS THE INNER DESIRE THAT KEEPS BOTH HE AND HIS CHARACTER COMING BACK FOR MORE.

AS BOLD AS BRASS

Even if he wasn't starring in the world's most popular crime franchise, chances are you'd recognize Paul Guilfoyle. After all, this is an actor with 90 movies to his name, including such celluloid classics as *L.A. Confidential*, *Quiz Show* and *Wall Street*. When the 58-year-old Guilfoyle finally hangs up his acting boots however, it's as Captain Jim Brass that he'll be remembered, at least by *CSI: Crime Scene Investigation*'s legion of fans. Over the course of eight seasons, Guilfoyle has taken a character who was fairly unlikeable in the first few episodes, and transformed him into a multi-layered human being, one that you can both sympathize with (especially in the case of his daughter Ellie), and rage against.

Here, Guilfoyle chats about his time on the show...

What first attracted you to the role of Captain Jim Brass?

As an actor, I liked the style of the show, especially the idea of the flashback. It had the feeling of an Akira Kurosawa movie. Until this point I had been doing films, but my wife was pregnant and I was about to have a child, so I wanted to get a regular television show, one that I felt had some resonance.

I don't so much find a role attractive. I see characters as vessels, things to be filled up with courage and fear and authenticity. That's what I bring to the table. I could see that Jim Brass was an opportunity to do that.

Brass isn't the nicest of characters in those early

episodes. Did you deliberately play him that way?

For me, Jim Brass is a bank account that I've been investing in a little at a time. When I read that first script it wasn't a case of me saying, "Wow, this character is all there, I hope I can live up to it". The character was actually fairly clichéd. I had to find a way around that and bring out the human being.

Jim Brass isn't the most likeable of guys in the beginning. But I realized it's because he's miserable – he's not doing the job he wants to do. In that first episode, Brass is the head of the CSI lab, because that's how it's authentically done. He's very abrupt and mean with this new CSI, Holly Gribbs, just because his own arrogance gets in the way. As soon as he returns to being a detective, he turns out to be

a different kind of person right away.

Eight years is a long time to be on one TV show, what is it about Brass that keeps you interested?
Brass is good at his job and he's very smart at his job in a way that only detectives who know the streets can be. He has a great sense of irony and humor and is a very nimble thinker. On the surface, Brass looks like an old-fashioned guy, not the sort of person you'd expect to have a tattoo. He looks like a cop and acts like a cop, but he has these other aspects that are surprising. The guy plays the cello, but he's also capable of telling some pretty nasty jokes. People don't act like they look, and I enjoy bringing these sort of surprises to the role.

The nature of his job sees Brass confronting the worst humanity has to offer on a daily basis. How do you feel he shakes that off every morning?
In real life we spend most of our days doing our jobs, trying to avoid tragedy and maybe enjoying a little comedy along the way. We don't want to be confronted with death and dying. We don't want horrific events to happen to us. That goes for policemen too. They try and process things straight away, they don't want to connect with every single criminal. If they did, they'd be an emotional wreck, they couldn't do their job. That's part of the secret of Jim Brass – he's a real guy. He can't possibly enter into the mind of every criminal. He protects himself.

With nine regular characters, it's inevitable that Brass will occasionally take a back seat. Do you ever find yourself wishing you had more screen time?
I'm a pragmatist about it. After all, the show isn't called *Jim Brass* is it? I'm pretty sure it's called *CSI*, which means it's about the ensemble, and I'm happy to

my God, what a perfect person. I even joke with Billy about it. He's better than Sherlock Holmes!

You talk with such pride about *CSI*'s ensemble cast. Do you feel this is the reason the show remains as popular as it is, even after eight years of airtime?
I think it's a very big factor. In television, you have to flow with the current. You can't just present the television show you have in your head – you have to go with the path of least resistance. The people who make this show, people like our executive producer Carol Mendelsohn, really have their fingers on the pulse. They saw that people liked each other and worked well together, and they let this ensemble grow and drift. It came together organically.

You still sound so enthusiastic...
This is my job, not my life. I'm an actor, I like doing it, and I know how to do it. I find ways to challenge myself in the midst of anything that's given to me.

The season six two-parter *A Bullet Runs Through It* is a highpoint in the *CSI* canon. What are your memories of these episodes, particularly that wonderful final scene?
Because of the way our schedule worked, one episode was directed by Danny Cannon, a guy from London, and the other, Ken Fink. These are two of our best directors, really wonderful guys. Both very different, but both absolutely good at what they do. For me, *A Bullet Runs Through It* was one story, so there was the issue of not having one person to rely

> "When storylines focus on Brass you see how inadequate he is. I would like to see more of that in Gil Grissom. I mean, my God, what a perfect person. He's better than Sherlock Holmes!"

report that we have a wonderful mix of actors and crew.
It's a bit like being in a band, where everyone has a role to play. No one person is in the forefront, and I think this is a testament to Billy Petersen who comes from the theater and has a love of ensemble work. He doesn't want it to be all about Grissom and I wouldn't want it to be all about Brass. Every once in a while to have a story about him? That makes sense. Mostly when the storyline focuses on Brass you see how inadequate he is. He isn't able to overcome everything by himself. I would like to see more of this in Gil Grissom. I mean,

WHO ARE YOU?

JIM BRASS PROFILE

After all that Captain Jim Brass has been through over the past eight years, it's a wonder the ex-Marine manages to show up for work each day – but then again, work is the closest thing Jim now has to a family. Divorced, Jim learns in *Ellie* (2.10) that his one child is not his biological daughter – worse still, her biological father is a 'dirty' cop from Brass's old beat in New Jersey. His relationship with Ellie starts poorly and gets worse – when she first appears, brought in as a suspect in a homicide in *Ellie*, she spits on her father's badge; she is later shown to be working as a prostitute, and only calls Brass to ask for help when a fellow working girl goes missing in *Hollywood Brass* (5.20).

A new low is reached when Brass is fighting for his life in *Way To Go* (6.24), having been shot in the chest. Ellie attends the hospital, only to try and scam the keys to his home and cash-in his pension. When recovered from his chest wound, in *Built To Kill, Part One* (7.01), Brass gets the date of the shooting tattooed next to his scar: 'May 11, 2006'.

In the *Pilot* (1.01), Brass is demoted from CSI supervisor to detective, after the death of CSI Holly Gribbs, with Grissom taking over the role. The tension this causes between the two eventually dissipates; when Brass is in hospital, it's revealed that he's given power of attorney to Grissom instead of Ellie. In some ways, being shot could be seen to be redemptive for Brass, after his involvement in the 'friendly fire' death of Officer Bell in *A Bullet Runs Through It, Parts One & Two* (6.07 & 6.08).

THE WIT AND WISDOM OF JIM BRASS

"I think every new hire should experience an autopsy on their first night." – *Pilot*

"Ring any bells? Rub-a-dub-dub. Dead man in a tub." – *Anonymous*

"Whoa, whoa. What, you start the party without me? That could get dangerous." – *Justice Is Served*

"Ellie, why do you do this to yourself? You're better than that. You're better than him." – *Ellie*

"A plus B plus C equals 9-1-1." – *Burked*

PAUL GUILFOYLE'S SCREEN CREDITS

Over the course of a 30-year career, Paul Guilfoyle has been in more than 90 movies. Here's a selection of his best work...

Tempesta (2004)
– as Taddeo Rossi
An American art historian travels to Venice to value several prestigious paintings, but soon finds himself caught up in a web of intrigue involving expert art forgers. Paul plays a millionaire art enthusiast.

In Dreams (1999)
– as Jack Kay
Neil Jordan's psychological thriller in which a troubled woman has a premonition of a young girl being murdered. Paul stars as a sceptical police detective (sound familiar?).

L.A. Confidential (1997)
– as Meyer Harris 'Mickey' Cohen
Oscar-winning thriller about the seedier side of American law enforcement. Paul stars as the head of an organized crime ring.

Extreme Measures (1996)
– as Dr. Jeffrey Manko
A doctor suspects foul play at the hospital where he works. Paul plays "the head of the emergency room".

> "Brass is good at his job and he's very smart at his job, in a way that only detectives who know the streets can be."

on, but I actually think both directors did really remarkable jobs. Danny put in a very intense interrogation for me in the first episode, and Ken expanded that final scene in a very beautiful way. It was only supposed to be a small, very little scene.

I felt there was a spiritual quality to that final scene, with Brass trying to find forgiveness for this guy's death. That was a great example of actors and directors working well together.

What would you like to see happen to Jim Brass in season eight?
I'm always seeking to give Jim more autonomy in the interrogation room, so viewers can really see the smart way he gets characters to unravel. I think it's interesting to see a person break someone down, especially in the casual way that Brass does it, which is part of his skill.

Jim Brass isn't exactly the luckiest of characters. Would you like to see him catch a break in the near future?
I certainly wouldn't want anything to happen to him. I think Jim Brass seems to fall into holes and then gets resurrected. He's been shot, he's been tattooed and his

daughter is a real mess. But every time he falls down, he struggles back and that's not a bad arc to have. If you're going to leave a little scribble in the sand as an actor, then the idea of bringing yourself back up isn't a bad one. You know, to realize you're in freefall and hit the bottom, but then to bring yourself back up to a place where you can find your humor and irony again.

One final question, the CSI franchise is watched by an incredible two billion people in 200 countries. Is there, in your experience, such a thing as a typical CSI fan?
I'm always amazed by the variety of age groups that approach me. And also the fact that they approach me as if they know me, or rather as if they know Jim Brass. When I was in movies they'd approach me as an actor – they were approaching the racing driver. Now they approach the car. This television show for one reason or another has struck a chord. CSI

DIY CSI
ODONTOLOGY

YOU WILL NEED:

Ever wondered how CSIs match teeth marks and impressions? Here's our beginner's guide...

AN APPLE OR ANOTHER SUITABLY HARD-FLESHED FRUIT, SILLY PUTTY, THREE FRIENDS.

Odontology deals with the proper examination, handling and presentation of dental evidence in a court of law. An odontologist's work can cover identification of remains through dental records, or through testing of the teeth themselves, as well as bite mark analysis, and age estimation. Tooth enamel is the body's hardest substance; teeth are often the last remnants of a decomposed body and dental records and remains are the quickest way of identifying an unknown victim. A trained odontologist will be able to take dental impressions from suspects and victims in the field, which can be used for comparison at a later date. All mouths are as unique as fingerprints, and can be identified by up to 76 comparison factors including indentations, chips, abrasions, and tooth width and alignment. If you've ever wanted to know who's been eating your food, here's how you do it...

HOW TO...

In order to compare bite marks you need a sample for comparison. Have one of your friends secretly take a bite out of an apple. Make sure it's a clean bite, showing a curved impression of the teeth. Roll the silly putty into three smooth, flat rectangles, at least the width of a bite, and distribute them among your three friends. Everyone should then bite down onto the putty, but not hard enough to go all the way through.

When all the impressions are done, line them up next to the sample bite, and try to match the impressions. Look for any tell tale signs, including chips, alignment and tooth size. Do you know which of your friends tasted the forbidden fruit? CSI

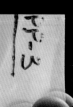

TOOTH 0746
FEB 16 2001
PORTIA RICHMONDS BEDELIA
G.GRISSOM

WEIRD SCIENCE

→ ON THE SCENE

IDENTIFICATION OF HUMAN REMAINS

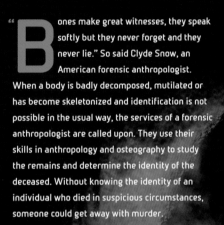

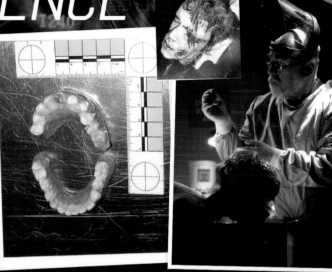

"**B**ones make great witnesses, they speak softly but they never forget and they never lie." So said Clyde Snow, an American forensic anthropologist. When a body is badly decomposed, mutilated or has become skeletonized and identification is not possible in the usual way, the services of a forensic anthropologist are called upon. They use their skills in anthropology and osteography to study the remains and determine the identity of the deceased. Without knowing the identity of an individual who died in suspicious circumstances, someone could get away with murder.

THE 'JIGSAW MURDERS'

On September 29, 1935, a young tourist came across a grisly scene. Under a bridge on the banks of the Annan River in Scotland, she saw a human arm protruding from a small bundle. Forensic experts were assembled and 70 body fragments were found in similar bundles, some downstream from the bridge

and others in areas further away. The fragments were sent to Edinburgh University where they were painstakingly reconstructed by Professors John Glaister and James Couper Brash. They concluded that the pieces belonged to two women, one aged between 20 and 21 and about 4'10" and 4'11" (1.47-1.51m) in height, and the other probably between 35 to 45 years of age and about 5'3" (1.61m) tall. Insect larvae and other incidental evidence placed the time of death at 12 to 14 days earlier.

The disappearance of Mrs Isabella Ruxton and her maid Mary Jane Rogerson on 14 September was then linked to the case. The physical attributes of the reconstructed bodies matched those of the missing

women, and photosuperimposition of one of the skulls showed a particularly close match to Mrs Ruxton. Furthermore, both bodies had been mutilated specifically in those parts that bore identifying marks, such as scars and birthmarks. The mounting evidence led to the arrest and trial of Dr. Buck Ruxton. He was found guilty of the murder of his common-law wife, Isabella, and the maid, Mary, and was hanged on May 12, 1936. He admitted his guilt before his execution.

The case was widely reported in the press and the success of the methods used led to increased public and professional trust in the capabilities of forensic science in the identification of human remains and in solving crimes.

→ ON THE SHOW

How identification techniques proved vital in helping Catherine and Warrick catch a family of lawbreakers...

Catherine and Warrick are called in to investigate a dead body found in a storm drain in *Down The Drain* (5.02). As they are climbing out of the sewer, they are approached by a Streets & Sanitation worker who has found some bones down another drain. After setting up a filter in the drain, a rib bone is found and Catherine determines that it is definitely human. The sewers are then flushed and the almost complete skeleton is found under a manhole in a residential street. Doc Robbins reassembles the body and concludes that the person was male, at least 5'6" (1.7m) tall and that he was stabbed from behind at least twice. When the dental records show that he was a teenager, Catherine and Nick do a search of the missing persons database. Estimating time of death to be about two to three years previously, they come up with a large number of possible hits. Meanwhile, Grissom is doing an experiment to determine how long it would have taken for the body to decompose – he discovers that the body could have been down the drain for as little as five weeks. With this information, Nick can now narrow the search and he finds a likely match in Travis Giles. After questioning people in the residential street,

Brass is directed to the Durbin house. Sara and Warrick then find blood spatter on a closet door in the house – as well as a number of pipe bombs. The bomb squad is called and the CSIs are forced to leave. Once the explosives have been cleared, the team moves back in. They find more blood spatter at the top of and going down the stairs and a hidden box of neatly-folded clothing. Grissom then discovers a knife stuffed behind the refrigerator. Unfortunately, the bomb squad discovers that the refrigerator is full of liquid explosives. They have to detonate them and the knife and other evidence is lost. Travis's grandmother brings in one of her grandson's baby teeth. From this, the CSIs match the blood in the Durbin's stairwell to Travis. Owen Durbin, a local bully, claims it was an accident; that Travis fell on the knife. But Catherine states that this isn't possible as the bones show that Travis was stabbed from behind at least twice. Brass accuses Mrs Durbin of the murder – only a mother would neatly fold the victim's clothing. Owen becomes enraged and threatens to kill Brass and Catherine. He is charged with murder, Mrs Durbin is charged as an accessory and Mr Durbin is charged with possession of explosives.

CRIME EVIDENCE

TOOTH ___ 0766
Article ___ Exhibit No.
FEB 16 2001
Date Found, Located or Developed
PORTIA RICHMONDS BEDRM
Where This Article Was Found
G. GRISSOM
Investigation Officer

PIECING IT TOGETHER

The identification of human remains is an important part of the postmortem examination and absolutely essential when the death is suspicious. In most cases, bodies can be identified by a close relative or friend, but sometimes, when a body is badly decomposed or there is extensive mutilation, this isn't possible. Other methods are then used and other features are looked at by forensic anthropologists or pathologists. The features used to identify a non-skeletonized body include:

Height – this is found by measuring the length of the body from the crown of the head to the heel. Post-mortem changes mean that this may differ slightly from the height of the person when they were alive.

Weight – estimating this is problematic as bloating associated with decomposition may lead to an overestimation of the person's weight before death.

Age – red 'Campbell de Morgan' spots found on the skin and a white or grey ring around the iris could indicate old age. For those under 25, the pattern of growth of the teeth can be used to estimate age.

Eye color – this is useful in identifying Caucasians, but only in the first few days after death. After this time, decomposition makes all irises appear brown.

Hair color, structure and distribution – color may be useful but it can be affected by decomposition, and hair can, of course, be dyed. The structure of head hair may indicate racial origin, while facial hair may assist in identifying the sex of the deceased.

Skin pigmentation – this may be of some use, however decomposition can significantly alter skin color.

Facial appearance – photographs of the face may be circulated to obtain a possible identification but this is only possible if the body is not noticeably decomposed.

Fingerprints – these are taken in the same way as from a living person, although in some cases the removal of the skin is required. To avoid contamination, fingerprints are taken at the end of the postmortem examination.

Other external features – personal features like tattoos are useful as they may still be seen even after the outer layer of the skin has been lost. Scars are also particularly helpful if they can be checked against medical records or verified by a relative. Other external features that aid in identification include skin blemishes, pierced body parts, and amputated limbs.

Internal examination – this may reveal medical conditions, such as heart disease or previous surgery. Comparison with records of possible matches may then assist in the identification process.

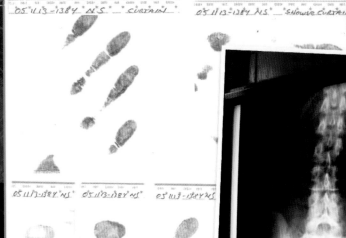

THE BARE BONES

Through natural decomposition, the soft tissues and organs eventually disappear to reveal the skeleton. If a collection of bones is found, it is important to establish that they are in fact bones and that they are human. Once this is verified, the process of identification can begin. This includes:

Height – if the skeleton is complete, direct measurement, taking into account the loss of soft tissue can be used to determine height. An approximation of stature can also be obtained by measuring from finger-tip to finger-tip of the outstretched arms, the span of which is roughly equal to body height. If the skeleton is incomplete then the major limb bones can be measured and the height estimated using the Dupertuis and Hadden formula.

Sex – differences between men and women can be seen in the pelvis, which is shallower and wider in females. The long bones in males tend to be more robust and the ridges that provide the connections to the muscles are more prominent. The skull is particularly useful in determining sex, with the female skull being smaller and more refined. In the Ruxton case, for example, Professor Brash was able to report that, "Secondary sex characters are so well marked that I can express without hesitation the definite opinion that it is the skull of a female."

Age – between the ages of 5 and 25, the fusion of the epiphyses can be used to estimate age at the time of death. The epiphyses are the growing ends of the long bones. These ends are soft and cartilaginous during the growing period but gradually harden and fuse to the main part of the bone when adulthood is reached at about 25 years of age. The pattern of the growth of teeth can also be used in estimating the age of people

who have died before the age of 25.

Dentition – teeth can provide the best means of individual identification. Postmortem examination of teeth and their comparison with dental records is usually done by a forensic odontologist.

Anatomical structure – the pattern of the frontal sinus is unique to each individual, and if X-ray information from prior to death is available, this can be used to confirm identification. Photosuperimposition and facial reconstruction can also be used.

Bone injury and disease – evidence of past injury and a number of disorders that affect bones may be useful to prove identification.

Surgical implants – the presence of an implant that bears a unique serial number may provide definitive identification of the person.

THE COMPLETE PICTURE

Once all the relevant information has been obtained, an assumption about identity is made. Discovering the identity of human remains is certainly not easy and mistakes can be made. Even in the celebrated Jigsaw Murder case, the body of Mrs Ruxton was initially thought to be that of a man as she was quite a well-built, stocky woman. However, in most instances, the expertise of the forensic anthropologist, pathologist and odontologist can be relied upon to make a correct assumption about identity. CSI

SECRETS AND LIES

As Jim Brass' bitter, wayward, and unforgiving daughter Ellie, NICKI AYCOX broke all our hearts. Here the in-demand young actress shares her season two memories...

Were you aware your *CSI* episode *Ellie* was the first time the series hit number one in the ratings?

I just found that out recently when I was shooting my new show with [longtime *CSI* director] Danny Cannon. I was in the dark all these years but that was great news to hear.

What immediately intrigued you about the character of Ellie Brass?

I've always been a huge fan of cop dramas so I loved *CSI* when it first came out and then the other spin-offs when they started. What appealed to me was getting the opportunity to play a character with substance. Ellie had a bit of a dark past that was linked to one of the main characters, which added some drama for him.

What conversations did you have with Paul Guilfoyle over the dysfunctional relationship between Ellie and Brass?

When I came in, Paul had a really good sense of what he wanted to do with the relationship from the father's side. To be honest, we were pretty much on the same page. He wanted to be a very giving and loving father who felt his hands were tied. Ellie had a troubled past and I concluded she would hold a grudge against him. That fit in quite nicely. He loved her and wanted to be a great father but his own problems and issues stopped him

short of that, not to mention the fact that Ellie wasn't willing to accept him as a father figure.

Did you nail that opening spitting sequence right off the bat?

That was a one-take thing. You bring up memories. *CSI* was one of the first roles where I had to do something of that nature to another actor. I remember being so scared about having to spit on Paul, but he was a great sport about it. He came out and said, "Just spit on me. Don't worry about it." I remember thinking this is the strangest job I've ever had, and did it.

Was that final goodbye between Ellie and Brass emotional to film?

I think it's more emotional for me now when I watch it as opposed to then when I was focused on what I was trying to get across on film. We had flown to Vegas to shoot those scenes. After we finished, I spent some time with Paul. He showed me around Vegas since I had never been before. Now when I see that performance, it really does come across as two people who care but can't make amends at this point in time. That's pretty sad, which is exactly what I wanted to get across.

How did the *CSI: Miami* episode *The DeLuca Motel* come about?

Actually, they called me up and asked

me to do it. I was out of town working so that was just something that came to me. I jumped at the chance because I was really excited to do another *CSI*.

What stands out about your time on *CSI: Crime Scene Investigation*?

My favorite moment was Paul teaching me craps in Vegas after we finished the episode. I tried my best but still never mastered it. I couldn't get the numbers straight.

Two projects you have in the pipeline are *Christina* and *The Line*. What are they about?

Christina is set in 1945 and is about a woman in Berlin who murders her baby because she wants to save the child from the war. It's very dark and sad. *The Line* [now called *Dark Blue*] is a Jerry Bruckheimer show we are doing on TNT. That was a lot of fun because I got to do some weapons training, drive around in a cop car, and wear a bulletproof vest. We shot the pilot in December and should be filming again in a few months.

Lastly, are you reprising your role as Minxie for *Jeepers Creepers III*?

That seems to be the question everyone's asking. I've talked to director Victor Salva about it but nothing is set in stone. CSI

"I re member being so scared about having to spit on Paul, but he was a

great sport about it. >>>>>>>> SEASON >

2

CASE FILE
Classic *CSI* episodes revisited!

EPISODE:
A Bullet Runs Through It,
Parts One & Two (6.07 & 6.08)

FIRST SHOWN (US):
November 10 & 17 2005

FIRST SHOWN (UK):
February 27 & March 6 2006

WRITTEN BY:
Richard Catalani & Carol Mendelsohn

DIRECTED BY:
Danny Cannon (6.07), Ken Fink (6.08)

REGULAR CAST:
Gil Grissom (William Petersen)
Catherine Willows (Marg Helgenberger)
Warrick Brown (Gary Dourdan)
Nick Stokes (George Eads)
Sara Sidle (Jorja Fox)
Capt. Jim Brass (Paul Guilfoyle)
Dr. Albert Robbins (Robert David Hall)
Greg Sanders (Eric Szmanda)

GUEST STARS:
Alex Carter (Detective Vartann)
Conor O'Farrell (UnderSheriff McKeen)
David Berman (David Philips)
Gerald McCullouch (Bobby Dawson)
Wallace Langham (David Hodges)
Ty Upshaw (Officer #1)
Larry Mitchell (Officer Mitchell)
Louise Lombard (Sofia Curtis)

A BULLET RUNS THROUGH IT
Parts One & Two

SYNOPSIS, PART ONE

A running gun battle across 20 blocks leaves three suspects and one cop dead, one teenage bystander badly wounded, and a mile-long crime scene to process. Witnesses in the Hispanic neighborhood where the shootout ends report seeing police fire on one suspect who had his hands in the air to surrender; the father of the wounded boy claims the police shot his son and sues the department. The CSIs determine that a fourth suspect shot the boy and made a getaway on his bike – but when they find and arrest him at a local motel, he's assassinated by a sniper before they can get him into a patrol car. Worse still, when Doc Robbins concludes the autopsy on slain Officer Bell, he discovers the cop was shot by "friendly fire" – another officer. Suddenly Brass and Sofia are the suspects in his killing...

SYNOPSIS, PART TWO

An investigation into the events that preceded the firefight uncovers a drug connection – a pregnant woman seen on CCTV being bundled into one of the suspect vehicles is proven to be a drug mule, carrying narcotics in a fake belly. She and her partner refuse to name names when questioned; even with the prospect of a lengthy jail term, they would rather serve time than incur the wrath of the cartel. Sofia is devastated to learn she may have shot Officer Bell but, due to it being an internal matter, is unable to find solace in her friends at the department – she shouldn't even discuss the case with fellow suspect Brass. The search goes on for the missing bullet; when it's found, blood confirms it as the fatal shot but it's too damaged for a comparison to other rounds. Instead, Grissom, Sara and Nick perform a laser reconstruction to replicate the trajectory of the shot and determine the identity of the shooter.

A problem shared: Brass attempts to comfort Sofia.

THE SCIENCE

The car Officer Bell was in had taken 78 shots alone; when Nick finishes putting trajectory rods in all the holes, he notes that it "looks like a porcupine". Rifles, AK-47s and handguns were all deployed during the gun battle, leaving hundreds of bullets and casings for the CSIs to process, to tell them who shot who and where they were standing at the time.

Gun barrels leave distinct markings called 'striations' on the bullets that pass through them, making it a relatively simple job to compare a bullet from a crime scene to one fired under controlled conditions in the crime lab from a suspect weapon. (Of course, it's possible a criminal could have changed barrels before being caught, which would make it impossible to link a crime-scene bullet to his weapon.)

At scenes where bullets are too damaged for comparisons, the ballistic trajectory can tell investigators a lot about a crime and its perpetrator. In this instance, a dummy representing Officer Bell is placed at the centre of the scene, while Grissom, Sara and Nick use laser pointers to link up Sofia and Brass's positions to the final resting place of the bullet, inside a nearby house. It becomes apparent that, even if Officer Bell had moved, one of the suspects couldn't have had a clear shot, making the other culpable.

X marks the spot: Grissom attempts to determine who shot Officer Bell.

FROM SCRIPT TO SCREEN

In a candid interview, episode co-writer and former crime scene investigator RICHARD CATALANI reveals the inspiration behind the gripping A Bullet Runs Through It two-parter...

Where did the idea for *A Bullet Runs Through It* come from?

The idea behind *A Bullet Runs Through It* was a compilation of three or so cases that I worked on. The last 10 years that I worked in the crime lab I worked in the Firearms Identification section, commonly called Ballistics. I used to go out and investigate the shootings and collect the evidence and analyse it. We were very busy; we got called out a lot and had a lot of officer-involved shootings. So I had a lot of experience with those types of shootings. I combined three of those stories into *A Bullet Runs Through It*.

Can you elaborate on those three stories?

On one of the cases there was an officer-involved shooting that started with the officers involved attempting to make a car stop for some reason. Another car pulled in between the cops and the car they were attempting to stop and the occupants pulled out AK-47s and started shooting at the cops. So they, of course, forgot about the original car and were preoccupied with having their ass shot off by these other guys. A chase ensued and the cars crashed. They had a big shoot 'em up and three of the four bad guys got killed. So that was the beginning of it...

In the process I also included a couple of really curious firearms cases I worked on. I had more than one actual case where the cops face off against the bad guy and become so focused on the bad guy's gun that they end up shooting the gun and hitting it. So we made some interesting circumstances around that.

The last aspect was another real case where the bad guy's running and they always try and ditch their guns. So they throw them up on roofs, hoping they won't be found. This bad guy threw his gun on a roof, then stopped and put his hands up because he knew he was going to get caught anyway, so he didn't want to get caught with a gun. So in the process, the gun slid off of the tile roof and the bad guy – human nature being what it is – caught the gun! So now he's a guy with a gun and the cops shot him. So that was a real case.

Why a two-parter?

We pitched the story and Naren Shankar, our executive producer, kept saying, "This could be a two-part episode". So we continued the pitch and he said it again. So it went from being one story that had too much stuff to contain in it to a two-part episode. CSI

ZINGER, PART TWO – Grissom: "We have reason to believe that Officer Bell was killed by friendly fire. It was a through-and-through and we haven't recovered a bullet yet – it's a big crime scene." UnderSheriff McKeen: "Unacceptable. Get back out there and find that bullet, I don't care if it takes everyone you've got, working around the clock." Grissom: "I said we haven't found it yet. I didn't say we weren't looking…"

Deep in thought: Brass and Grissom survey the scene.

"Moustache boy!"

TRIVIA

● The title of the two-parter is a play on the name of the 1992 Brad Pitt drama *A River Runs Through It.*

● Warrick is the first to point out the change in Nick's appearance when he calls him "moustache boy" in the locker room. For reasons unknown, Stokes appears in these episodes with a hairy top lip, causing great consternation on messageboards the world over. Thankfully, it's long gone by *Still Life* (6.10).

● These episodes mark the first time lab technician Hodges attends a crime scene.

CHARACTER DEVELOPMENT

Sofia Curtis is a relative newcomer to the LVPD, first joining the department early in season five. A detective turned CSI turned detective again by the time of these episodes, Sofia has not experienced a fellow officer being shot dead before and finds it hard to cope with the knowledge that she might have fired the bullet that killed Officer Bell, whose wife is heavily pregnant with their third child. She tries to speak to Grissom but Sara intervenes – she's on administrative leave and prevented from discussing the investigation with anyone in the department – leaving Sofia alone with the guilt that, as she confides in Jim Brass, "I'm always going to be the cop who shot a cop". But did she?

PLAYING WITH FIRE

IN AN EXCLUSIVE INTERVIEW, ACTRESS MARG HELGENBERGER TALKS ABOUT THE TRIALS AND TRIBULATIONS THAT HELPED SHAPE THE FIERY CATHERINE WILLOWS...

→

> ## "I fought to keep Catherine as an ex-stripper. I thought that was another way of keeping her femininity."

Procedural dramas are nothing new but ever since *CSI: Crime Scene Investigation* debuted in 2000, processing evidence, deciphering clues, and outwitting the bad guys has never been cooler. Naturally, the top-rated series' slick style and gripping crimes are integral ingredients to that increased interest, but there is no denying it is the engaging actors and their flawed characters that make the journey so compelling. In fact, it is almost impossible to imagine anyone else but the Emmy-nominated actress Marg Helgenberger portraying feisty investigator Catherine Willows.

"*CSI* itself was intriguing because it was the first time a show had featured the criminalists," says Helgenberger. "In the past, it has always been the cop or the detective. This time, it was the people who did the collection and analysis. Also, the style was intriguing. All of those, what are now known as *CSI* shots, were written into the pilot script. That is what made the science exciting, fun, and why it captured viewers of all ages. I don't think anyone anticipated this show was going to have such a broad mass appeal. It has influenced young people to become criminalists and made them fascinated with science because it was made to look fun."

A Vegas girl through and through, there is more to Catherine than simply beauty and brains. A former exotic dancer, it was her baggage, tenacity, and spunk that truly clinched the deal for Helgenberger.

"The character interested me because on the page, she was described as CSI level 3, single mother, and ex-stripper," she recalls. "I thought there were enormous amounts of things to play with because even when you are solving crimes, it informs the character. When the pilot was picked up, before we started our new season, the producers had lunch with me and thought they might do away with the ex-stripper aspect of the character. They created this whole other scenario for her and I couldn't even tell you what it was because it was so uninteresting. I was able to fight to keep, and win, that part of her back story."

WHO ARE YOU?

CATHERINE WILLOWS PROFILE

CSI supervisor Catherine Willows is Las Vegas royalty. The daughter of a showgirl and casino magnate Sam Braun, she simply wouldn't exist if it weren't for Sin City. Finding out Sam was her father was bittersweet for Catherine – she knew he and her mother, Lily, had a relationship but it wasn't until Braun was inextricably linked to a bloody bank heist (*Inside The Box*, 3.23) that she had cause to compare DNA. Hers had seven alleles in common with a suspect, making Sam both her father and a killer. Alas, Catherine's CSI instincts worked against her – although she cracked the case, she'd done so by unconventional means, so the case against Sam for the murder of cocktail waitress Vivian Verona was dismissed (*Assume Nothing*, 4.01). The father-daughter relationship would become further strained when Sam started dating Lily again, although Catherine would eventually accept a $250,000 check, which she put towards sending hard-to-handle teenage daughter Lindsey to private school.

Despite being beautiful, smart and successful, Catherine has nothing but trouble with men. Her unreliable ex-husband, Eddie, was shot dead by a shady associate, leaving her to raise Lindsey alone (*Lady Heather's Box*, 3.15), while potential partners met through work inevitably turn out to have criminal tendencies. An ongoing flirtation with fellow LVPD CSI Warrick Brown, most notably in *Down The Drain* (5.02), was the closest Catherine seemed to get to a new romance – but Warrick's hasty marriage put a stop to that. When Sam's shot dead after a campaign of violence (against Catherine, who fears she's been raped) and Lindsey (who's kidnapped; *Built To Kill*, 7.1-2), Catherine realizes how much she's lost – and that Grissom is the one man she can rely on.

Having Catherine modeled after Las Vegas criminalist Yolanda McCrery gave Helgenberger a unique insight into the rigors of the profession and its daily grind. "I would have to say spending time with Yolanda on ride-alongs to crime scenes and being part of the whole process really helped," agrees Helgenberger. "One of the crime scenes was a dead body in the Hard Rock Hotel. There were no suspicious circumstances involved and I ended up going to the autopsy of that person the following day. I spent a lot of time with Yolanda and I think along with Robert David Hall, we were the only two cast mates who witnessed an actual autopsy."

Sadly, forensics is often considered a boys' club and although Catherine is as tough and resourceful as any of her male counterparts, it is always tricky depicting those qualities without losing her softer side.

"You have to be very strong and I even saw some of that behavior with Yolanda," explains Helgenberger. "You almost have to go overboard but she didn't really; she was just herself. Yolanda was so together, smart,

WILLOWS TALK
Remember these?

"Stick with it. At least until you solve your first. And if after that, you don't feel like King Kong on cocaine? Then you can quit. But, if you stay, with my hand to God, you will never regret it."
– [Catherine to Holly Gribbs] *Pilot*

"You two ladies done talking?"
– [to Gil Grissom and Jim Brass]
I-15 Murders

"So, let's get to know each other. You first. You were born, you came home from the hospital. Then what?"
– [to Roy Logan]
The Finger

TRIVIA
Marg won an Emmy Award for her role as a tough prostitute in the TV series *China Beach*.

and focused. She takes enormous pride in her work. That was the other reason I fought to keep Catherine as an ex-stripper. I thought that was another way of keeping her femininity. One can still be sexy without compromising your work habits."

FAMILY TROUBLES

Catherine might have a knack for solving crimes but her family life is a mess. At best, her relationships with rebellious teenage daughter Lindsey and casino mogul father Sam Braun have been stormy and shaky.

"I'm sorry Sam is not alive anymore because we had such a complicated relationship," offers Helgenberger. "Then there is the fact he was a casino boss. We've alluded to that at the beginning of this season, in which I've basically inherited the land my father's new casino was to be built on. By the end of the season, Catherine is going to have to make a choice about whether she wants to continue being a criminalist or perhaps move on to being a casino owner. I am interested to see what they are going to do [with that storyline]."

Her unlucky streak was also apparent in *Weeping Willows* where Catherine had a flirtatious encounter with a man, Adam Novak, who later became a suspect in a double homicide. Played by Helgenberger's real life husband Alan Rosenberg, the character returned once more in *Leaving Las Vegas*.

"I have talked to a lot of people who have worked opposite their spouse," smiles Helgenberger. "Obviously, there is an enormous amount of history that you don't have to work at because it is automatically there. There

> "Our stories are so dark that I really look forward to the ones that are more comic and have a lighter tone to them."

is a bit of taking each other for granted which wouldn't exist with someone you just met. And there isn't the excitement if you just met, especially if it is a charged relationship, whether it is sexually or anger. In the case with Alan in the first episode, that was the situation. It was an attraction which led to what I thought was a fatal attraction which I doggedly try to overcome."

Perhaps Catherine is looking for love in all the wrong places. After all, with all the subtle glances, fans assumed she and Warrick Brown would have hooked up by now.

"First off, I have known Gary [Dourdan] for a long time," says Helgenberger. "We did a pilot together about five years prior to *CSI* so we already had that automatic history and mutual admiration. And we do have chemistry so I kept encouraging that. The writers would tease the audience or us with it and then would back off. I am not exactly sure why they did that instead

of following through. Now that everyone is aware of that relationship between Sara and Grissom, I don't think they would probably go down that road again with another character. It remains an open field."

Catherine's darkest hour came in season seven's *Built To Kill* two-parter where she was drugged and then victimized by men seeking to get back at her father.

"That idea was mine," reveals Helgenberger. "It came from a conversation I had with Yolanda. She and some girlfriends had been to a bar in which they had heard the bartenders were being paid off to slip date rape drugs into the girls' drinks. The girls had been drugged and who knows what else had happened to them. I thought it was an interesting way to approach a woman who is usually always watching her back and not getting herself into a situation, that it would happen to her, how she would cope with it, and when she would

TRIVIA

During the very early stages of her career, Marg was a weathergirl for a news channel in Nebraska, going by the name Margi McCarty.

tell her co-workers. I thought they did a really nice job of arcing the story."

During Grissom's teaching sabbatical that year, veteran CSI Michael Keppler joined the gang, frequently teaming up with Catherine, and obviously making a strong impression on the cast. "That was great, not only to have a shake-up with the new blood, but they wrote him very heavily and why wouldn't you utilize a newcomer and someone of Liev Schreiber's talent?" says Helgenberger. "It was thrilling and he is a writer so he contributed a great deal to his character and the arc of the story. It was almost like you were shooting the first season in that it was always, 'What do you think of this? Let's try this.' Liev had such enthusiasm, and he is a great guy. He doesn't have a lot of hang-ups like some actors. I was really sorry to see him go."

In *Redrum*, Catherine agrees to Michael's unconventional plan to smoke out a killer, a strategy that required Catherine to deceive her co-workers.

"Those actions were justified but Catherine didn't have a choice," reasons Helgenberger. "It came down from above that this is what they were going to do to shake out a suspect who had gone underground. And the whole time she hated lying to her team mates, but it paid off in the end."

EIGHT EXPECTATIONS

So far, season eight has seen Sara Sidle leaving, David Hodges becoming a more prominent presence in the lab, and the introduction of eager young investigator Ronnie Lake. Change can be good, although sometimes all that reshuffling can come across as being too fast and forced.

"I will be frank with you; I don't think this has been one of our better seasons," offers Helgenberger. "In the 11 episodes we have done so far, I think they were just throwing things out there. Obviously, Jorja Fox had chosen to leave. The way they ended the Miniature Killer and having her leave was well executed. It was a good idea to bring in another new face and Jessica Lucas was adorable, but I just don't know if her character worked well in the mix of things. With the wrap up and departure of a very popular character, we were just starting to get our footing when the strike happened. I am very curious as to what is going to happen [with the rest of the season]."

Despite Helgenberger's concerns about season eight, there have been some real gems this year, such as *The Chick Chop Flick Shop*. "There was a scene in that episode I really liked which was the spoof on the B movie horror film," enthuses Helgenberger. "It was

MARG HELGENBERGER'S SCREEN CREDITS

Marg's most memorable TV and movie moments...

Mr. Brooks (2007)
– as Emma Brooks
Marg plays the wife of serial killer Kevin Costner in this well-received psychological thriller.

Erin Brockovich (2000)
– as Donna Jensen
Starring alongside Julia Roberts (who won a Best Actress Oscar for her role as Erin), Marg stars as a victim of chemical exposure.

E.R. (1996)
– as Karen Hines
Marg played George Clooney's love interest (lucky thing) for five episodes in the long-running medical series.

Species (1995)
– as Dr. Laura Baker
Classic sci-fi/horror movie in which Marg plays one of a team of doctors who create a dangerous human/alien hybrid, which then proceeds to wreak havoc on L.A.

really fun, kitschy, and that writer, Evan Dunksy, always writes those offbeat whimsical episodes. Our stories are so dark that I really look forward to the ones that are more comic and have a lighter tone to them. There was a scene with a dwarf who was coming on to me that was a lot of fun to play."

Other highlights over the years include showcasing a vulnerable Catherine as well as just acting opposite her co-stars. "The two premiere episodes [from season seven] where I am slipped the roofie and that whole story that ended with my father being shot in my arms was really intense," offers Helgenberger. "I also certainly enjoyed working with Liev. And any time Billy and I have scenes to do, it is magic because we like and respect each other so much. The first two seasons we were together so much and then they realized they needed to give us a break so we don't solve many crimes together anymore. I miss that." CSI

DIRTY ROTTEN SCOUNDREL

One of season three's biggest dramas was the death of Catherine Willows' slimy ex, Eddie. TIMOTHY CARHART, the actor behind the man who created many a headache for the CSI team talks about his time on the show...

Let's get one thing straight right from the start: Eddie Willows might have been a thorn in the side of Marg Helgenberger's Catherine, but the man who plays him couldn't be more charming and friendly, as well as being blessed with an extremely wry sense of humor (as you'll see from reading this interview).

Since starting his career in 1978, Carhart has appeared on hundreds of TV shows and many movies. Those of you obsessed with *Ghostbusters*, for example, might recognize him from a fleeting appearance as the violinist friend of Dana Barrett (Sigourney Weaver) who gets roundly insulted by Bill Murray's Peter Venkman. Surprisingly, for someone who has made a career out of his acting skills, the profession didn't grab him at an early age: "I was never infected with the acting bug fortunately and my whole family has been vaccinated, although we worry about the mercury," he jokes. But he does credit the traveling his family did during his youth as helping him lock down characters. "I find that living among other cultures can, in the right person, create the empathy necessary to inhabit another person's soul." Yes, even if that soul is for a character like Eddie.

And so to *CSI*, where Carhart spent three seasons occasionally popping up as the charming-yet-sleazy ex-husband of Catherine Willows. As with most actors who play bad apples on screen,

he found something to love about Eddie, even though he admits the character turned rotten quickly.

"Eddie started out as a loveable rogue and turned into a pathetic schlub rather quickly, I thought." Yes, he spent three years either plotting to wrest custody of daughter Lindsey from Catherine or getting mixed up in dodgy dealings. It's not every character that's introduced in the middle of a rape case, after all.

After a brief audition process, Carhart landed the role of Eddie, and started with the first season episode *Who Are You?*, which saw him arrive on the scene in the middle of the aforementioned case. "I was offered the part with the understanding that it would be some kind of story arc. When Marg fell in love with me, of course, it expanded into much more." Yes, despite their fraught relationship on screen, Carhart and Marg Helgenberger clicked right away. "She was very much the seasoned professional. She has such a hypnotic quality and I was instantly smitten," he says, before cracking. "Unfortunately, they didn't allow us to consummate our relationship on set for contractual reasons!"

His time with *CSI* came to an end brutally in season three with the episode *Lady Heather's Box*, which found Eddie murdered and Catherine broken up over the lack of evidence to convict his killer. "I guess that I had a couple weeks' notice

that my character would be killed. I used all of my time practicing bleeding," smiles Carhart. "When the day came, I spent hours lying in the gutter, bleeding all over the place, wet, with the producer leaning over me asking me what it was like to be the new guy on *24*. Delightful!"

Despite the violent end to his tenure on the show, he has happy memories of his time providing problems for the Las Vegas crime team. "Compared to my other credits, working on *CSI* was delightful. The entire cast couldn't have been nicer or more supportive.

"Especially Marg, who I am sure went to bat many, many times to try to keep me on the show and in her character's life," Carhart continues with another smile. "For that I will be forever grateful to her."

Though his character was the sort of schmuck that fans love to hate, Carhart usually has positive encounters with viewers, and they often express their desire to see Eddie and Catherine end up happy, despite, you know, the death thing. "Mostly when I see fans on the street they tell me that, above all, they wish with all their hearts that Catherine and Eddie would have renewed their vows at the Circus Circus casino's miniature putt-putt attraction, and had loads more children," he jokes.

Yet while some deceased *CSI* characters – most notably Rory Cochrane's Tim Speedle on

"Eddie started out as a loveable rogue and turned into a pathetic schlub rather

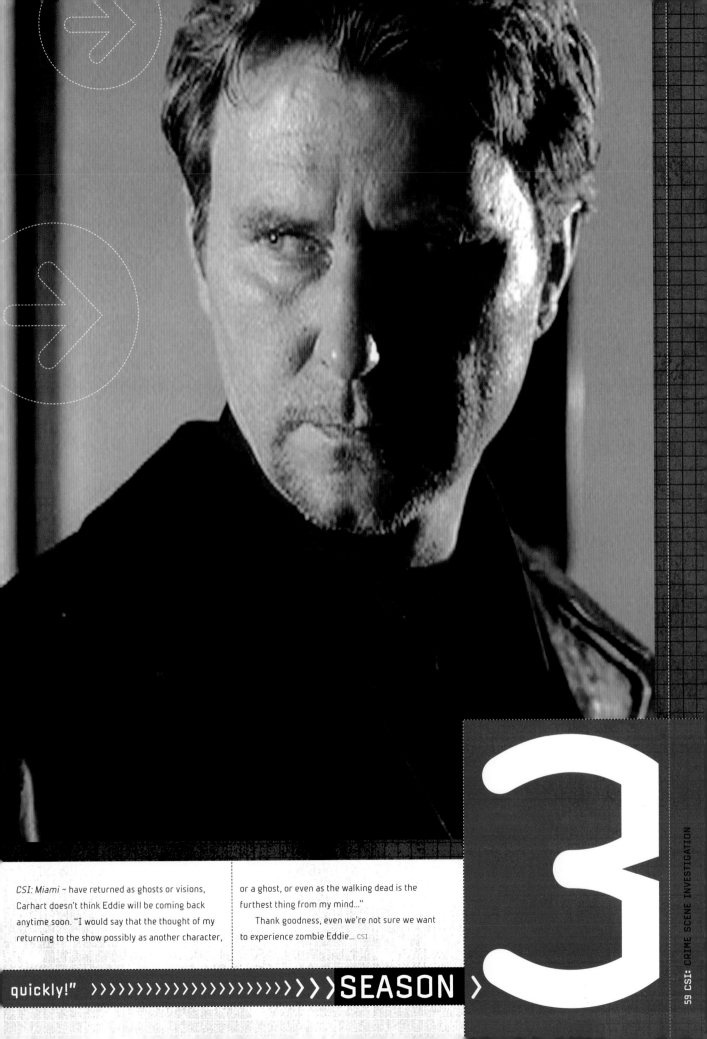

CSI: Miami – have returned as ghosts or visions, Carhart doesn't think Eddie will be coming back anytime soon. "I would say that the thought of my returning to the show possibly as another character, or a ghost, or even as the walking dead is the furthest thing from my mind..."

Thank goodness, even we're not sure we want to experience zombie Eddie... CSI

quickly!" 〉〉〉〉〉〉〉〉〉〉〉〉〉〉〉〉〉〉〉〉〉〉〉SEASON 〉

3

FINAL DESTINATION

They say an apple a day keeps the doctor away, but no amount of fruit is going to save you if you find yourself on the table in Doc Robbins' morgue. Meet *Robert David Hall*, the actor behind TV's quirkiest coroner...

62 CSI: CRIME SCENE INVESTIGATION

DO NOT CR

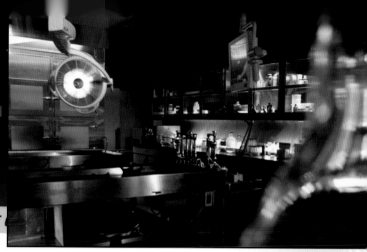

TRIVIA

Robert had both his legs amputated in 1978 after being crushed by an 18-wheeler and suffering burns over 65% of his body.

N ow in his eighth season playing LVPD medical examiner Doctor Al Robbins, actor Robert David Hall admits to enjoying the role as much now as he did when he first joined the cast in the sixth episode of *CSI: Crime Scene Investigation*'s first season – especially since the writers have really begun to explore the character's quirkier side. In an exclusive interview, the 60-year-old actor, who really is the nicest of guys, talks us through his favorite *CSI* memories, as well as revealing what it's like to be an actor of disability in Hollywood...

What do you make of the ongoing success of *CSI*?
The joke on set is that when you get old and go to a retirement home the only thing you'll be able to see is *CSI*. [Laughs]

Did you have any idea it would become the phenomenon it has when you joined the cast?
No. Most actors live hand to mouth and it's pretty rare to have regular work, and I thought, "Wow,

if this goes two or three years that would be incredible," and now we're working on our eighth season. And we're still pretty popular in the ratings, we're in the top five all the time. It's one of those things where you try to be aware of it, but not dwell on it.

My wife didn't think the show would last a year [laughs]. Thank God she didn't have great judgment! I just try to go in there and have fun. I've been through worse things than a show being cancelled but that's the last thing on anybody's mind with *CSI*. The writers and the chemistry of our cast keeps it interesting.

Does the show's popularity ever become overwhelming for the actors?
We just go in and learn our lines and do our stuff. It's quite amazing. I've been acting a long time and it's strange still to be noted on the street. They may not know exactly who you are, but they know you're the guy, the doctor. Most people are very kind about it, they want to tell me that their son is studying chemistry or that their daughter wants to be a criminologist, and I find that quite interesting.

It's not just America where the show is a success either, is it? It's huge all over the world...
I love the fact that what we do translates in so many cultures and I'll tell you, American TV doesn't translate as well as it used to. I mean Western people could get the mythology, it was

POLICE LINE DO NOT CROSS   POLICE LINE DO NOT CROSS   POLICE LINE DO NOT CR

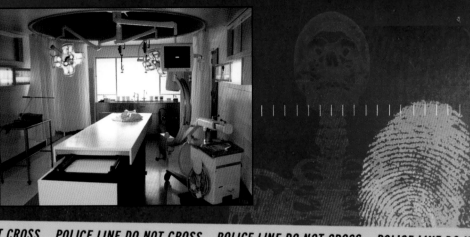

CROSS   POLICE LINE DO NOT CROSS   POLICE LINE DO NOT CROSS   POLICE LINE DO NO

"I'm in my early 60s, and all my cousins are getting ready to retire but I want to act until I'm 95!"

like Kurosawa, part of every country's myth, the loner lawman or something like that, but things that are uniquely culturally American didn't necessarily work overseas and suddenly our show comes along and once again there's an American show. I'm not waving a flag, I'm just saying it's unusual that an American show is so well received and mesmerizing to people. I love it. I've had kids come up to me in Italy saying, "Dottore Robbins! Dottore Robbins!" I had to say, "Hey, ciao bella, I don't speak Italian!"

Did you always want to become an actor?
All I wanted to do [when I was growing up] was play music, listen to music, read books and travel. I went to UCLA while the Vietnam War was going on – I must have taken seven majors in six years to get through college and then I bummed from Amsterdam to Egypt and back and spent about a year and a half living in Spain for two months, Greece for two months, Morocco for two months, Italy, London. I worked in Paris hanging up burlap walls and playing in bands in the Metro. A lot of American kids had these groovy, "I don't want to grow up," fantasies and

ultimately, sooner or later, everybody has to grow up to some degree, unless you're an actor. And that's why I chose this profession. You're going to get your chance to be happy and your chance to suffer and if you can die having had 51% of happy versus 49% suffering, you're a lucky person!

What attracted you to the role of Doc Robbins in the beginning?
A job, it was literally that. I happen to be a man of disability [Hall lost both his legs in a car accident in 1978] and, as an actor, especially a male

actor, all I would get offered would be the occasional auditions for the role of the angry crippled man, or something like that. As I got older somebody said, "Well, let's throw a robe on him and make him a judge." So I did every TV show that had a judge in it, and a couple of films. I tend to play the crusty doctor, professor, judge...

I like to make every role I play believable, so [when I got the part on *CSI*] I did a little research. I talked to my family doctor, who knew a guy, who knew a medical examiner, so I went and talked to him before I even did my first episode. I thought they were all ghoulish, strange people but,

LICE LINE DO NOT CROSS   POLICE LINE D

"If you had an airplane pilot, you'd want it to be Billy Petersen. He looks like he could land the 747."

in fact, he was a professional medical doctor who had gone into forensic speciality years ago. [Having seen him work] I tried to play the character very straight in the first few episodes.

You were originally only hired for one episode. When did you know you would be returning to the show on a regular basis?
I think when I finished my first scene, William Petersen had already decided that I would be the regular coroner, although they didn't tell me that for quite a while. So one episode turned into two, they asked me back a third week and then a fourth, suddenly I was there for 15 episodes the first year and still thinking, "Man! This is great, 15 episodes!"

Then at the beginning of the second season they made me a regular and, at the beginning of the third season, they put my face on the front of the show and for an actor this is a great thing. I never expected this thing to pay off. I'm an actor because, like every other moron actor before me, I jumped off this cliff without a parachute and I said, "Uh-oh, I guess you can't go back." All my friends are musicians, dancers, actors, and I have my cousins who are lawyers and naval officers. I mean, I'm in my early 60s, and all my cousins are getting ready to retire but I want to do this until I'm 95! This is fun. I'd like to be the mad scientist in a great movie in 2030. It's a wonderful profession that I'm in.

What's it like working with William Petersen?
He's a straight shooter. To use a rugby or football analogy, he's the captain of this team. I'll tell you how I see it. A lot of actors think they can rewrite a script, they'll say, "I don't want to say this line, I want to say this line, this sucks, I want to change this!" Almost everybody who does that I have some problems with. When Billy makes a suggestion, it's almost always for the betterment of the scene. In addition to his acting, he's pretty straightforward – if he says something he does it, and he doesn't promise the moon. He's an executive producer as well as the star of the show. Women

like him, men like him. I'm the eldest of five kids, I never had an older brother and he's not older, I'm older than him, but if I had an older brother, he's the kind of guy I'd like to have! He's kind of a football playing, horseback-riding straight arrow sort of guy, he's not a goodie-goodie, but he's capable. If you had an airplane pilot, you'd want it to be Billy Petersen with one of those silly hats on. He looks like he could land the 747. Isn't that what it's all about?

Do you ever find yourself wishing your character had more screentime?
All of us actors have egos and I'm looking forward to what I do after *CSI*, but right now *CSI* is the number one thing for me. When you go to your job, the lighting people, the camera people, they're all our friends. We've worked with most of them for eight years now. I'm only guessing but I'd say that 70 per cent of our crew this year has been with us from the beginning. And that is unusual.

The show deals with the darker elements of modern life. Are the storylines a bit tough to take sometimes?
Yeah, we have our share of dominatrixes, or what's the plural – dominatrices? – and cross dressers and sicko killers and everything, but people are fascinated by this stuff, and TV and movies gives a safe distance from things that scare you. People like to be scared and grossed out with the safety of the tube between them. I don't know about you but I've actually witnessed some autopsies and I'm awfully glad I'm an actor! I admire the people that do this for a living but it's just something I couldn't do – the smell alone. If *CSI* were in smell-o-vision we'd all be in trouble.

In the season seven episode *Lab Rats*, Doc Robbins demonstrates an abject fear of rats. Is this a phobia you share in real-life?
No, I'm not truly terrified of rats, but I thought it might be a nice quirk. And they let me sing too. Some shows try to immediately develop the

WHO ARE YOU?

DOC ROBBINS PROFILE

The king of the backroom boys, chief medical examiner Al Robbins is the first person the CSIs contact when a dead body is brought back to the lab. He's had the odd honor of performing autopsies on both rapper Tupac Shakur (COD: respiratory failure and heart attack due to multiple gunshot wounds) and John Entwistle (COD: heart attack due to the effects of cocaine on a pre-existing heart condition), bassist with The Who – coincidentally the band responsible for the *CSI* theme music – and takes pictures of all dead celebs that grace his mortuary. It's this light-hearted approach to death – he also keeps a coffee machine in the morgue and plays in a band with the day-shift coroner – that enables him to do what he does, dissecting everyone from elderly adults to newborns to literally get to the heart of what killed them. In *Who Are You?* (1.6), Al's very first appearance, he spotted a hairline fracture in the skull of a skeleton encased in concrete, and salt and sand in the ear cavity – tiny, seemingly insignificant details which lead the CSIs to discover that Fay Green was battered in the living room of her lover's house, complete with tropical fish tank, by her jealous ex-partner. Al's mother believed his interest in death came as a result of his being the twin of a stillborn baby – as Las Vegas legend Elvis Presley was. (The loss of both his legs, in a car crash, can only have increased his gallows humour.) Oddly, while death holds no fear for him, the same cannot be said of rats; when a sizable rodent emerges from the corpse of a drowning victim in *Lab Rats* (7.20), Al dons a heavy-duty Hazmat (hazardous materials) suit and insists his assistant coroner, 'Super Dave' Philips, does the same...

CRIME SCENE INVESTIGATION

characters and I think *CSI* very wisely has been slow to reveal things about the personal lives of our guys. They've also hinted that I have a wife and three daughters, and that I raise cats and dogs. I think in one episode to relieve stress I visit a strip club, but they dole it out in such small amounts that the audience fills in a lot of the blanks themselves.

Finally, we've heard your great story about when Quentin Tarantino directed the show. Any more on-set tales you'd like to share?
Quentin Tarantino? I had the most fun I've had on this show [when he directed]. He's got to be 42 or something, but it was like we were all in junior high school – we were so mischievous. Usually you're used to directors being very serious and saying, "Now because this is a very wild scene, we have to play it very straight." Tarantino was like, "Let's go NUTS!" and it was great. I love the rhythm of our regular guys, but it's fun to break things up once in a while. CSI

ROBERT DAVID HALL'S SCREEN CREDITS

A selection of Robert David Hall's best work...

The Gene Generation (2007)
– as Abraham
Sci-fi thriller about a new breed of killers known as DNA Hackers, who hack their way into people's bodies and kill them. Robert plays the mysterious Abraham, alongside *CSI* guest star Faye Dunaway.

The Practice (1999-2000)
– as Judge Bradley Michaelson
Playing a high-powered judge, Robert guest-starred for four episodes of the popular legal drama from *Ally McBeal* creator David E. Kelley and starring Dylan McDermott and Lara Flynn Boyle.

Starship Troopers (1997)
– as Recruiting Sergeant
Robert attempts to persuade idealistic (and extremely pretty) teenagers, including Casper Van Dien, to sign up for a brutal war against giant bugs in this full-throttle sci-fi shocker from *RoboCop* director Paul Verhoeven.

DOCTOR IN THE HOUSE

Doctor Al's orders...

"It's a wild animal covered with potentially biohazardous material, with claws. Rabies, scabies, AIDS, hepatitis, I'm thinking of this suit as a giant rubber glove."
– Lab Rats

"When I was in fourth grade, I dropped karate because some kid half my size made me cry."
– Blood Lust

"You say tomato... I say cause of death!"
– Fight Night

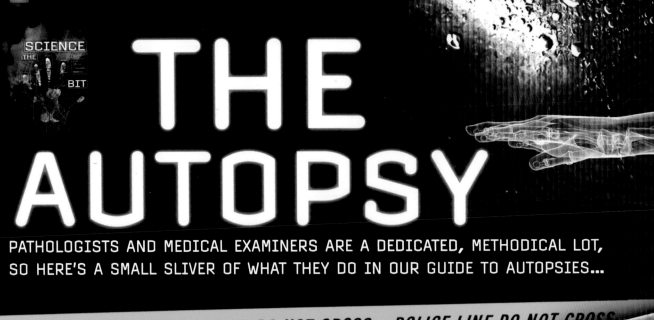

THE AUTOPSY

PATHOLOGISTS AND MEDICAL EXAMINERS ARE A DEDICATED, METHODICAL LOT, SO HERE'S A SMALL SLIVER OF WHAT THEY DO IN OUR GUIDE TO AUTOPSIES...

LINE DO NOT CROSS   POLICE LINE DO NOT CROSS   POLICE LINE DO NOT CROSS

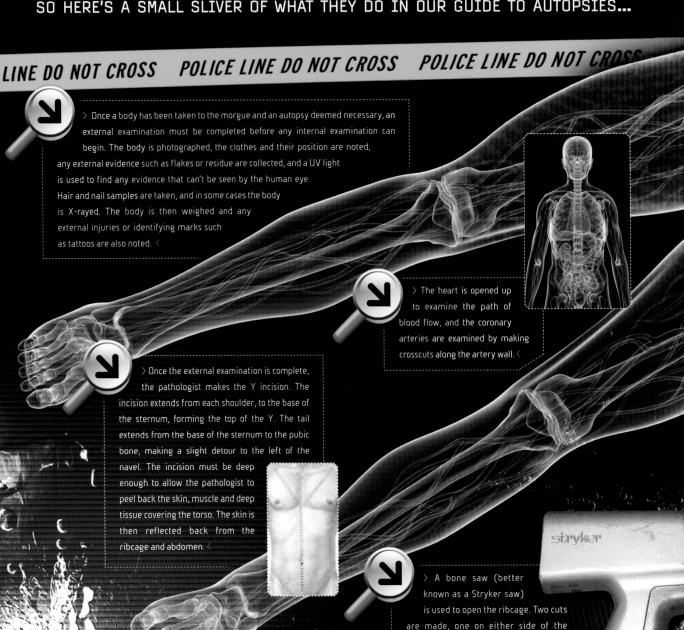

> Once a body has been taken to the morgue and an autopsy deemed necessary, an external examination must be completed before any internal examination can begin. The body is photographed, the clothes and their position are noted, any external evidence such as flakes or residue are collected, and a UV light is used to find any evidence that can't be seen by the human eye. Hair and nail samples are taken, and in some cases the body is X-rayed. The body is then weighed and any external injuries or identifying marks such as tattoos are also noted. <

> The heart is opened up to examine the path of blood flow, and the coronary arteries are examined by making crosscuts along the artery wall. <

> Once the external examination is complete, the pathologist makes the Y incision. The incision extends from each shoulder, to the base of the sternum, forming the top of the Y. The tail extends from the base of the sternum to the pubic bone, making a slight detour to the left of the navel. The incision must be deep enough to allow the pathologist to peel back the skin, muscle and deep tissue covering the torso. The skin is then reflected back from the ribcage and abdomen. <

> A bone saw (better known as a Stryker saw) is used to open the ribcage. Two cuts are made, one on either side of the ribcage to allow the chest plate to be completely lifted away, exposing the lungs and pericardial sac. The abdominal muscles are then reflected back to expose the stomach and intestines. <

stryker

> The stomach is opened and any contents saved for testing. The kidneys, bladder, and, in female patients, the ovaries and uterus, and the internal surfaces are examined. <

NOT CROSS   POLICE

> The organs are typically removed in one block. This is achieved by dissecting the organs of the neck – larynx and trachea – and continues downward, detaching the organs from the spine. Once all spinal connections are severed, the pelvic ligaments are cut and the organs are removed – very carefully... <

> Once the organs have been separated and weighed, the lungs, liver and spleen are cut into 1cm-thick slices for testing and closer examination under a microscope. <

> The skin of the scalp and face is reflected away after an incision running from one ear, across the crown of the skull and down to the other ear is made. This incision must be deep enough to allow the skin to be pulled down over the face in one direction and away from the skull towards the neck in the other. <

> Once all of the organs have been removed and prepared, and the pathologist is satisfied that no further evidence can be gleaned from the body, the Y incision is closed, as is the incision across the scalp. In some cases the remains of the organs are placed back in the body, otherwise they are incinerated at the facility. The slices for testing will go off to the lab. Once the incisions are closed, the body is released for burial or cremation. <

> A bone saw is then used to remove the top of the skull. The outer layer of the brain, the Dura mater, is attached to the cranium and is removed when the skull is opened. The spinal cord connection is severed and the brain lifted out. Due to the fragility of the brain, it is placed in a jar of formalin for a minimum of two weeks before further testing can be done. <

– With thanks to Ed Uthman

POWER STRUGGLE

HE'S THE MAN *CSI* FANS LOVE TO HATE, BUT CONRAD ECKLIE HAS SHOWN A SOFTER SIDE IN RECENT SEASONS. ACTOR MARC VANN EXPLAINS WHY THERE'S MORE TO THE ASSISTANT LAB DIRECTOR THAN VANITY AND AMBITION...

Tension between Grissom and Ecklie was tangible since day one. What were your first impressions of Ecklie and his work ethics?

Well, just from the name Conrad Ecklie, I knew he was a prickly character and was probably going to be the nasty thorn in the rosebush. His work ethics were more by the book, hard-nosed, and at odds with Grissom's warm, paternalistic approach. Plus, there seemed to be professional jealousy and a competitive history present from the get go. There was lots of sports talk about "my team, your team."

Another thing that helped add to the immediate tension between the characters was the fact that Billy [Petersen] and I had done a play together in Chicago called *Flyovers* in the late '90s playing characters with an antagonistic relationship. It was set during a 25th high school reunion. Back in high school, his character was a troublemaker who used to bully and beat up my character, the straight As, slightly obnoxious, know-it-all nerd. Twenty-five years later, the bully is an unemployed factory worker and the nerd is a successful movie critic. The tensions we were able to tap into and develop in that play certainly helped define the Grissom/Ecklie relationship.

Back in season one, did you get the sense *CSI* would become this ratings juggernaut?

Not at all. I remember it was doing well on Friday nights and then CBS moved it to Thursdays. At the time, I thought that was insane. I've always felt the whole ratings battle thing was like a childish schoolyard pissing contest, but that shows you how much I know about good business decisions. The move to Thursday was when *CSI* went off the charts. I think its success probably surprised a lot of people, as do most successes that are original creations and not part of some proven formula.

Nick once proclaimed, "I hate that guy!" Were you prepared to be the character everybody despised?

Yes. How can you not love to hate someone named Conrad Ecklie (laughs)? All those "k" sounds get right under your skin. And they didn't really have a jerk on the show. I think, originally, they may have wanted Brass to be a heavy but they turned that around pretty quickly, mainly because you can't really have a series regular be too much of a jerk

unless it's a comedy. I also didn't know how much they were going to use me so I just resolved to play him as big of an asshole as I could muster, just in a quiet way, which is my style.

Deep down, do you believe Ecklie split Grissom's team into shifts to spite them?

Deep down, yes. However, he completely justified his actions and would never admit that to anyone or even to himself.

Despite the animosity, were you pleased that Ecklie pitched in when Nick was buried alive, or recently with Warrick's troubles?

I really don't think Conrad is a bad person. He is just filled with insecurities, jealousies, and power needs which manifest themselves in passive-aggressive behavior. When it comes to life, death, and doing the right thing, he's going to come through. I think Conrad is quite capable of heroic behavior.

What kind of direction do you get from a man like Quentin Tarantino, and what did you enjoy about the way they used Ecklie in *Grave Danger*?

The things I remember most about working with him was his joyous energy on set, how much the crew adored him, and how gracious he was when we first met. Quentin literally started acting out a violent scene I did on *The Shield* four years earlier in pretty remarkable detail and telling me how much he liked my work. It made me blush and put me immediately at ease. I later found out he did this with some other actors as well. It was a very generous gesture. I loved the way Ecklie was used in *Grave Danger*. He was being helpful and part of the team, especially in the scene where Conrad tries to get the Undersheriff to let the Lab generate Nick's ransom money through budget cuts, but the Undersheriff won't go for it. Conrad even offers to take the heat for it. Instead, the Undersheriff tells him to get his people ready for a funeral. It's the first time you see Conrad at least attempting to be a hero, when, up to this point in the season, he's been mostly a pain in the butt.

Over the last few years, Ecklie seems to have mellowed out. What do you believe was the turning point?

Well, certainly the near deaths of Nick and Sara, as well as the situation with Warrick, have matured him quite a bit. Once he got promoted to Assistant Lab Director and sat in that superior isolated position for a while, the mellowing process began. Obviously, right after the promotion, he was on a rampage and broke up the team in season five. However, once he embraced the responsibility of his new position, most of his behavior has been justifiable. Of course, he could backslide anytime.

Photo by @ Stephanie Howard

You've known Billy Petersen since your theater days – how has it been reuniting with him?
Fantastic. Billy is a great guy and an amazing actor, both on stage and screen, and I've personally learned so much about camera acting watching his work on CSI. He also embodies the ensemble work ethic so characteristic of Chicago theater. I believe that is one reason why "The Team" feels so authentically cohesive on the show.

As I mentioned, we did a play together in the late 90s, but before that we really did not know each other. He had seen me in a production of The Cryptogram at Steppenwolf Theatre. We met one night after that show and some time later, he was looking for someone to play the role of the movie critic in Flyovers. Apparently, I was on his short-list. Fortunately for me, it worked out. It was a very memorable theater experience to be onstage with him.

What's happening with Ecklie in season nine?
Conrad has really been shaken by Warrick's shooting. He had problems with Warrick from day one, mostly with his gambling and Grissom's unwillingness to appropriately discipline him and get him in line, but I think he always liked Warrick as a person. In some ways, Conrad may blame Grissom for what happened but he would never express that, mostly because he knows Gil holds so much guilt already.

Having been around since season one, what differences have you noticed now in terms of production compared to when CSI began?
When a show has been around for nine years, you've got to mix it up. I love how it has evolved and the different directions the writers have been willing to experiment with, such as exploring comedy, focusing on the lab techs, developing shows around subcultures that most people know nothing about, and expanding

the educational nature of the show. I love that kind of risk taking and it's one reason the show has preserved its high-ranking status. They have allowed DPs, and editors to direct. They have let directors, and recently one of my dear friends, Corinne Marrinan, who started season one as an assistant, write. It seems to be a loyal, collaborative environment that fosters newness.

Do you have any stand-out Ecklie moments?
Not really. I am very critical of my work, so I rarely am pleased with what I do. My proudest episodes were Mea Culpa and Iced. In Mea Culpa, I was able to explore Conrad's passive aggressive side. I had scenes with all the major characters and felt successful in making them different. Of course, that's the episode for which Ecklie is most hated. In Iced, I was the butt of a lot of jokes and had scenes with many of the smaller characters, which was a blast. It was great to explore Conrad's comedic potential and a lighter side. It's the different relationships that are the most fun part for me.

Have you ever had any funny fan encounters?
I was at a Jethro Tull concert once and I heard someone scream "Ecklie!" They then came up to me and proceeded to tell me very loudly how much they hated me. Early on, people would just stare at me with this look on their face like they smelled some rotten cheese. They couldn't quite place me but just knew they didn't like me for some reason, which puzzled them and deepened their frowns. Now, folks are nicer and generally place me rather quickly. Maybe they've forgiven me for breaking up The Team.

Lastly, from Lost to Angel to CSI, why does it seem you are the go-to-guy for these prickly characters?
In Hollywood, once you do something successfully, that's all people see you as until you are able to break

→ "Quotation"

> "Early on, people would just stare at me with this look on their face like they smelled some rotten cheese."

that mold. Talent buyers want to know what your specialty is, so they can put you in a box like a certain size piece of hardware for easy retrieval and sale. I've played a wide variety of roles on stage, but in TV and film, I'm in one or two boxes. Most stars manage to break out and do a variety of things but at my level, it's more difficult. Although, I do feel content just to have a niche. I would rather play bad guys, or characters with some kind of twist than anything else. They are always more fun. CSI

TRIVIA   Marc has been practicing yoga since 1998, and credits the exercise with helping him stay sane in Los Angeles.

SINS OF THE FATHER

As Sam Braun, SCOTT WILSON brought some old-school glamor to *CSI*, especially in season four when he gave Catherine $250,000. Here the actor discusses the show and his character's vintage Vegas style...

Sam Braun was a connected guy with a very murky past – was he based on any specific Vegas characters?

Some people think it was murky! The first season that I was there, I played a character that, I guess, was loosely based on Benny Binion – he was the owner of the Horseshoe club in Las Vegas in the 1950s – and that character was a family friend of Catherine's. The next season they called me and said, "He's a character we like, would you like to come back?" and I said, "Yes!" They have some great writers on the show, and they gave me some terrific scenes for him to play. It was fun. Coming back once a season meant I could re-think the character, and what had changed in his life.

Did you do any research into old-school Vegas guys when you took the role?

My research began years ago, when I used to go up to Vegas! When I first started going, the airport was just a hangar, with crop dusters. I won't say that I built those casinos, but I certainly paid for a table or two! I don't know that that speaks well of my gambling abilities... I shot most of my scenes in Las Vegas, and it's grown a lot and I don't think any of those original casinos still exist. When I would go to Vegas, way back, you'd kind of hear things – it's not really documented, but you would have an idea who it was about. But I think you had to do something really bad to upset those guys. It's

one of those things where I wasn't playing a real person so the research was about the legends – everyone knows the legends. I just played Sam like he wasn't a bad guy!

How would you characterize Sam's relationship with Catherine? Was the gift of $250,000 in season four a genuine gesture?

Oddly, they had a wonderful relationship before she found out he was her father! After that it became really tumultuous. I think Sam wanted to recapture that good relationship. I think there was a simple and true motive to the money – he was trying to win her back. He gave her a lot of money later on as well, when Nick was kidnapped. I love working with Marg. Most of my scenes were with her, and she's just a wonderful actress, and a wonderful human being, as were all the cast members. Bill Petersen is terrific – I had a couple of scenes with him as well that season. I also worked with Bill years ago when we shared a little scene in *Young Guns II*...

Sam's ambiguity was one of his best qualities. How do you see him? Is he capable of murder?

I think we're all capable of it under certain circumstances. I don't know if Sam's capable of it or not, but there certainly is a dark side to him. He wasn't above the law – he was the law!

I think he's a wonderful character. I still get a lot of responses from people about him. It wasn't like I was a semi-recurring regular, I came back once a season, maybe two times in the last season. But my character was talked about in episodes he wasn't in, so it created the illusion that he was around more than he was! He's like a ghost, and they still talk about his influence. It's fun to be an actor when you're involved in stuff that people respond to, and they certainly respond to that show. Everyone I see talks to me about it. It didn't become a lifestyle or a change in lifestyle for me like it did for most of the cast, but it did have a positive impact on my life. I have good memories of being on the show – it's been interesting watching it become so successful.

Sam first appeared on *CSI* in season two, before finally bowing out in season seven. How did the show change over the years?

I wasn't someone who was in the eye of the storm, I was more of an outside-inside observer and it was interesting to see how it evolved. They're such a tight-knit group and they clicked right out of the gate. I'd come in and have to play catch-up! It was fun, I worked with some wonderful people, and they made me feel very welcome. I hope the show lasts as long as they want it to. CSI

"It's fun to be an actor when you're involved in stuff that people respond to,

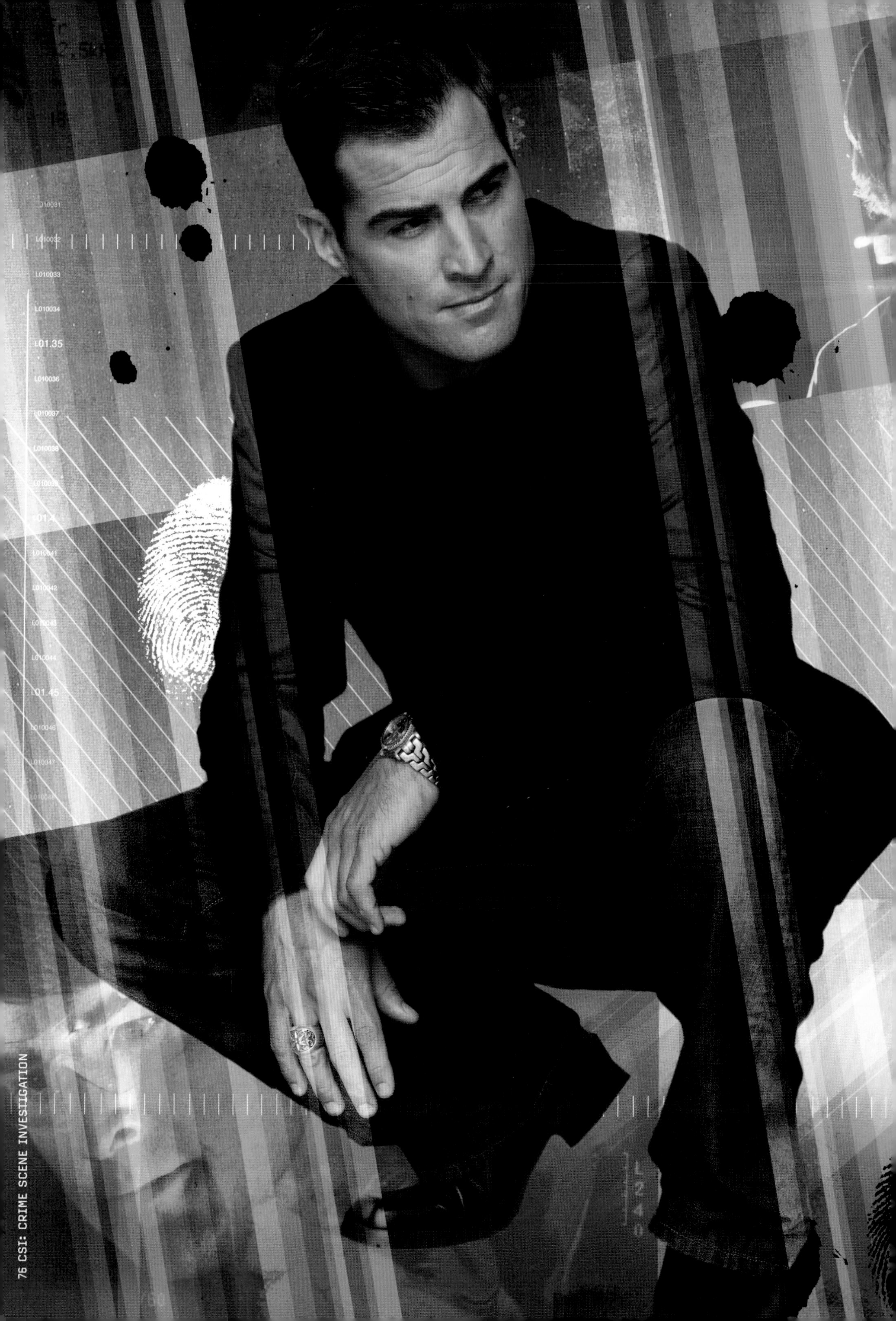

KISS AND TELL

There isn't much Nick Stokes hasn't done. With a degree in criminal justice from Texas A & M University, he spent three years on the Dallas police force before transferring to Las Vegas and becoming a CSI level 3. Ever since, he's been busy inspecting evidence, dusting for fingerprints, trudging through sewers, and dodging bullets. Solving bizarre and sometimes grotesque murders is all in a day's work for the hard-working CSI, and actor George Eads would have it no other way. With credits that range from the raunchy soap Savannah and the medical drama ER to the short-lived Grapevine, the immensely popular CSI: Crime Scene Investigation proved to be the opportunity of a lifetime for the Lone State star.

"I got lucky," acknowledges Eads. "You know, right place, right time. I got the news Grapevine wasn't going any further and I had a pile of scripts I was reading for audition, mostly TV because that had been my experience. I remember my manager asked, 'Have you read that Jerry Bruckheimer script?' I said, 'I didn't know CSI was Bruckheimer! Let me take a look at that!'

It was the last script I read and the last audition I had. When I went, they were seeing a bunch of guys, and I could sense their anticipation in getting the role filled."

After landing the coveted part, Eads immediately got an understanding of what kind of guy Nick Stokes was.

"Initially, we had a fake tattoo on my arm," recalls Eads. "They had wanted him to have some earrings and be rock and roll too. But I never really had the Paul Stanley hairdo I think they might have been looking for. I have this big square head. I thought, 'Wait a minute!' I had the tattoo, which took three hours to put on, and you can barely see it sticking out from under my sleeve in the pilot. I thought I had to amend this person because he is not how they thought he was going to be. I decided to have more of a jock attitude because you hadn't really seen a jock scientist before. It was comfortable for me and we kind of went from there.

"I remember in the second episode, we had these baseball hats and I'm wearing them to the set because it was an outdoor scene, and they freaked out. They were like, 'There are no baseball hats in TV. Nobody

Office romance. A kiss between Nick and Catherine was cut from the *Pilot.*

wears hats. No gum. No sunglasses.' I went to Billy's trailer and he's like, 'Man, you are a hat guy. That hat looks good on you. Wear it.' I'm like, 'Don't get me in trouble.' And he insists, 'Wear it!' So I wore it and almost got fired. I'm like, 'Thanks a lot dude!' But they ended up getting me special hats for the character to wear."

To prepare for such a meaty part, usually an actor will hit the books or shadow true CSIs, but if anybody knows about law enforcement it's Eads. As the son of a District Attorney, he used his father's experiences to influence his portrayal of Nick.

"What the occupation does to someone personally is more interesting than the science," offers Eads. "I am more interested in a marine's life away from the Marine Corps. What is a policeman like away from police work? Sometimes you see these guys are big

and it was just him and me. About five minutes before we closed, two guys came in and shoved guns in our faces. I was at gunpoint for what seemed like an eternity, especially since the guy's hands were shaking. His finger was on the trigger, and it was a revolver so you could see the bullets in there. I thought, 'He's going to slip. He's going to look the other way and blow my head off!' I remember everything flashing before my eyes – everything I had done and still wanted to do."

LADIES' MAN

With Nick's devilish grin, heart of gold and southern drawl, the CSI has never been short of female attention, even enjoying the odd flirtation with firecracker Catherine Willows (who's technically his boss). Early on, the sexual tension between the two characters was tantamount, and apparently there

> ## "I joke about that scene all the time: 'I want to make out with Marg, right now!'"

family people, but what about those other stories? Now, I'm not saying mine was a bad one, but my father was anything but perfect, and I think a lot of that had to do with the job. I try and put a lot of that into it. My Dad was kind of a Pit Bull to say the least. He really took it personally, especially if it was a heinous crime."

Furthermore, Eads had already had a scary dose of reality when he was held at gunpoint while working at a hamburger joint. "I was a short order cook while going though acting school," he reveals. "A buddy of mine owned a restaurant and I was helping to clean up one night. Back then, take home was probably $700,

were even discussions of them hooking up. "Yeah, actually in the first episode, even before Jorja Fox, they had Catherine and Nick meet in a drive through and make out while going through the case," reveals Eads. "But the dichotomy was weird so they ended up cutting it out. At the time I think they thought I had too much of a boyish quality. I joke about it all the time: 'I want to make out with Marg, right now!' The great thing about our actresses is they are really easy and fun to work with. If we started a storyline with Marg, I know she'd be all for it, but at this point it would seem weird."

"We did this scene where we are commenting on Grissom and Sara," Eads continues. "And I ask Greg, 'Did you know about the two of them the whole time?' And he's like, 'Yeah, I'm surprised you didn't.' He walks off and I go, 'That kind of grosses me out!' 'Cut! Don't say the grosses me out part.' 'All right, man. That is kind of creepy.' 'Cut!'

"At this point, I've even thought of pitching that it would be more fun for Nick to fall for someone in the line of work, maybe he comes across a child, goes to take him to day-care, falls in love with this woman who is taking care of all the kids, hasn't had time for herself, and he sweeps her off her feet."

Between being stalked and almost shot, Nick has also fallen victim to attackers on numerous occasions, but none were as traumatic as being buried alive in the season five two-parter, *Grave Danger*.

"It wasn't nearly as bad as it looked," remembers Eads. "I'd love to say I did my own stunts, got bitten by ants, and starved myself so I could lose 30 pounds. That just wasn't the case. There were about seven

THE WORLD ACCORDING TO NICK STOKES

"Blood's like my Grandfather. Never lies."
– *Friends & Lovers*

"Wait, wait. Time out, now. I had half a Caesar and a coffee. How's my end 20 bucks?"
– *Table Stakes*

"Tell me, am I radiating a green glow?"
– *Face Lift*

"Whoa, whoa. So she's not selling the organs on the black market... she's eating them?"
– *Justice Is Served*

"Sometimes I hate this job."
– *Burden Of Proof*

TRIVIA
When he first arrived in L.A. to become an actor, George could only drive during the day because the truck he'd borrowed from his stepdad had two broken headlights.

WHO ARE YOU?

NICK STOKES PROFILE

On the surface a happy-go-lucky Texan boy with few cares beyond solving his cases, CSI Nick Stokes has been the focus of more than one psychotic individual. Most infamously, he's the CSI who took the call to attend a faked crime scene in Quentin Tarantino's *Grave Danger* two-parter (5.24 and 5.25) and wound up buried alive until his co-workers linked Kelly Gordon to the crime and discovered the grave site at the garden centre where she worked. Glad to be alive, Nick even visited Kelly in prison but it didn't stop the crime haunting him – or her, as we learned when she resurfaced in *Daddy's Little Girl* (6.12).

In *Stalker* (2.19), Nick was pushed out of a second-story window and then had a gun pointed at him by crazed cable guy Nigel Crane. It wasn't the first time he'd had a firearm in his face – in *Who Are You?* (1.06), killer Amy Hendler threatened to make him her second victim. And it wasn't just his job that got him into trouble – aged nine, Nick was molested by a 'last-minute babysitter' and, until he confided in Catherine in *Overload* (2.03), he'd never told anyone about it.

Although he's been known to flirt playfully with Sara, Catherine and fingerprint tech Mandy Webster, Nick has never had a relationship within the lab – indeed, his only notable hook-up was with an off-duty hooker. He first met Kristy Hopkins in the *Pilot* episode (1.01), when she was doping clients in order to rob them; she then asked for his help in *I-15 Murders* (1.11) when she was booked for attacking a security guard. Nothing happened until *Boom* (1.13), when Kristy revealed she was giving up the game and they spent the night together. The next day she was dead, choked by her pimp. Ever the gentleman, Nick paid for a "proper burial".

different boxes, some with false sides, tops, and bottoms. There was one suspended in air."

He continues: "When I was saying goodbye to my family on the cassette, I imagined saying goodbye to *CSI*. It has been a big part of my life. When Quentin Tarantino started singing in my ears in a whispered hush tone, 'Hush little baby don't you cry...' it really gives you a green light to put your foot on the gas and go for it. I hoped it wasn't too over the top. The editors save us as actors because a lot of time I will try over the top, then subtle, then flat, and hopefully they will use different takes, which is what they did. And Quentin is such a cool guy. He would always come to my trailer in the morning, ask me how I was doing, if I was ready, and he would call me Nick on the set but George away from it. He just gives you so much confidence to do something maybe you didn't think you were capable of."

Previously, *CSI* consisted mostly of standalone episodes with a few lingering elements, but season seven broke that mold and ramped up the stakes by introducing the Miniature Killer, a devious adversary that consistently taunted the team throughout the year.

"I think it worked, and went above and beyond what I was expecting," reports Eads. "When I kept seeing different miniatures, I realized over five episodes it was starting to become a serial thing. It was a good time of the year for it because it was in the middle, and then we drew it out towards the end, but when we did revisit it, we didn't do it every episode. We would just do it sporadically, which is a good way to get people involved. A lot of stuff I question around here, which they welcome. I was like, 'The Miniature Killer is going to be a her? Aww man. Wait a minute!' In my mind, I expected it to be someone completely different, which is a tribute to our writers and creative team who sit around a big table to think about this stuff. They hired a really great actress so it starts with that. It just worked because it wasn't what we expected. Giving twists is what *CSI* is all about."

COMIC BOOK GUY

A ratings juggernaut with two spin-offs, *CSI: Crime Scene Investigation* has been further immortalized in other mediums such as games and novels, but none have tickled Eads' inner fan boy more than IDW Publishing's comic books.

"I really like them because the artwork is so well done and the stories are good too," he concludes. "I've tried to get every one I can get my hands on. I hope the time hasn't passed me by, but I still want to play a superhero. With the resurgence, it is starting to become old hat, but I used to read and draw those comic books for as long as I can remember. It had nothing to do with the movie *Spider-Man* or the TV series *Heroes*. I have superheroes in my home, like those miniature statues you get. They just fire me up and bring out the superhero in you. That is the feeling I've always had, that there is a superhero inside if I ever need him. Believe me, I'm past the point of envy, but to see Ben Affleck when he got *Daredevil*, I was like, 'Ooh, there goes another one!' And to see Tobey Maguire be tired of playing Spider-Man...

"It would be cool to have Captain America go back to World War II where he started and be him," Eads finishes. "That would be fun to have the leather mask, gloves, and the shield. On *CSI*, I continue to have that mentality with Nick Stokes, that he's this secret agent, this bad ass, and it is fun to have the liberty to play somebody who is kind of fearless. I put that vest on, those gloves on, the badge, the gun, and I feel like I am a superhero!" CSI

DIY CSI

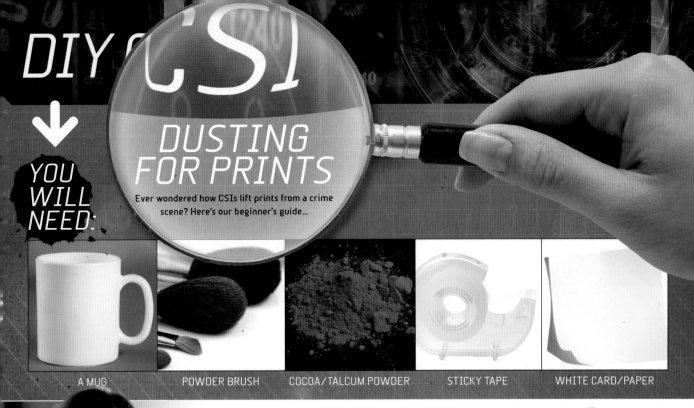

DUSTING FOR PRINTS

Ever wondered how CSIs lift prints from a crime scene? Here's our beginner's guide...

YOU WILL NEED:

A MUG	POWDER BRUSH	COCOA/TALCUM POWDER	STICKY TAPE	WHITE CARD/PAPER

As any good CSI will tell you, no two sets of fingerprints are the same, and as such they make fantastic identification tools. Every time you touch a surface you leave behind a unique and individual pattern, as a result of the natural oil secretions from your fingers. Prints are often latent, or invisible to the naked eye, and CSIs have several ways of revealing them.

The oldest and simplest of these techniques is commonly known as dusting. Prints left on shiny, non-porous surfaces such as glass are the easiest to recover, as these surfaces do not absorb moisture, leaving fingerprints intact. Household objects such as mugs work in much the same way, so if you want to know who has been using your mug while you've been on holiday, here's how you do it...

HOW TO...

To check a scene for prints, an investigator dips a fine brush in a jar of aluminum powder and very gently sweeps the brush over the surface they are examining. The powder adheres to the oils in the fingerprint leaving visible and traceable evidence of whomever touched the surface. However, if you can't get hold of any aluminum powder, cocoa powder does the job just as well. Lightly sprinkle the cocoa powder over the surface and gently blow the loose powder away.

Once an investigator has dusted a surface, any prints that appear are then very carefully lifted by pressing a piece of adhesive tape to the surface, being careful not to smudge or damage the print. The tape is then mounted on a piece of card or transparent sheet to preserve the print for analysis. To lift the print from your mug, place a piece of sticky tape over the print, carefully peel the tape back and stick it to a piece of white card or paper. If the surface you're printing is dark, talcum powder is a good alternative to cocoa, remembering to stick the print to a black piece of card.

Voila! You are now a fingerprint technician. Now all you have to do is look for a match... CSI

REASON FINGERPRINTED
✓ Prime Suspect

SOCIAL SECURITY NO. SOC
MISCELLANEOUS NO. MNU
REF

WEIRD SCIENCE

→ ON THE SCENE

FINGERPRINTING

$H2o2\ 2H2o$

Fingerprints... How many times have we seen Gil Grissom and his team come up trumps thanks to this simple method of identification? Here's a handy look at the history of fingerprinting, from the first successful conviction using the procedure in 1892 through to more recent breakthroughs in fingerprinting technology...

HISTORY BOOKS

Fingerprint evidence has been used successfully to ascertain guilt in criminal cases for over 100 years. The first documented success came in 1892, when, using the findings of eminent Victorian scientist Sir Francis Galton (who discovered that no two fingerprints were the same), Croatian-born Juan Vucetich proved a 27-year-old Buenos Aires woman had killed her two young sons. The woman had blamed the murder of the boys on a neighbor, but a bloody fingerprint at the crime scene proved her guilt.

Five years later, Galton's theories would lead to the foundation of the Calcutta Anthropometric Bureau (later renamed the Fingerprint Bureau) in India. In 1901, a fingerprint bureau was founded at the UK's Scotland Yard. The following year, the method was brought to New York.

TOOLS OF THE TRADE

To identify a fingerprint, first it must be recorded. A suspect in custody is 'printed' using inks or biometric technology, while at crime scenes, prints can be recovered from a variety of surfaces.

'Latent' prints are left behind by the skin's secretions (sweat, sebum, dead skin cells – which can sometimes also be used for DNA analysis) and are often invisible until detected. Powders and brushes are the most common way to detect a fresh fingerprint on a non-porous surface. A CSI would typically dust an area where a fingerprint

Brush with death: These days CSIs use aluminium powder to 'recover' prints.

would likely be found, then lift the print using sticky clear plastic strips that are then attached to card, making the print easy to photograph, scan and analyse.

On a porous surface, or when a fingerprint is more than a few days old, a chemical such as ninhydrin (or 'Triketohydrindene hydrate') can be used, which reacts with the nitrogen compounds present in fingerprint secretions to turn an invisible print purple. An 'Alternative Light Source' or a laser can also be used, which, when

the wavelengths are tuned correctly, can make invisible prints luminescent.

Sometimes, CSIs get lucky and prints are already visible. 'Patent' prints are those left behind in a substance (such as paint, ink or blood), which is easily photographable. 'Plastic' prints are ones left in a malleable substance, such as clay, soap or wax. Plastic prints are usu[ally] photographed and swabbed too, in case DNA evidence has been left behind in the ridge deta[il] that could also aid identification.

ON THE SHOW
How fingerprinting helped the Las Vegas CSIs get their man...

The first ever episode of *CSI: Crime Scene Investigation* features a fingerprint left at the scene of a staged suicide. This print leads Grissom to Paul Millander, a costume maker who cast his own hand for a prop. Grissom concludes that the print was faked and Millander was framed because the print they recovered contained latex particles matching the prop hand. Seven episodes later, a similar suicide scene is discovered and the same Millander print recovered – beneath a planted impression of Grissom's thumbprint. Grissom's response? "I get it. Whoever it is, is telling me that he's got me under his thumb." When the new victim's cash card is used to withdraw money, footage from the cash machine camera shows a homeless man holding up cue cards to taunt the CSIs. When brought in for questioning, the homeless man identifies Paul Millander as the man who paid him to put on the show – Grissom was tricked.

A year later, a third staged suicide is discovered. A series of speeding tickets issued to the dead men lead Grissom and Catherine to traffic court judge Douglas Mason – who appears to be Paul Millander. Grissom manages to lift his prints from a prison-cell bar but they match the prints on file to the judge, not to Paul Millander. The case appears lost until the CSIs visit Millander's mother and discover that it was his father, also called Paul, who used his hand to make the cast and whose prints were all over the crime scenes, not his son. Judge Douglas Mason and the young Paul Millander are the same person.

"Fingerprint evidence has been used to ascertain guilt for over 100 years."

BUMP AND GRIND

After recovery, the identification of a fingerprint depends upon the classification system in use. Under the Henry Classification System, three main types are identified: the arch (a small bump at the centre of a print), the loop (a much higher bump, starting and ending at the same side) and the whorl (a self-contained swirl shape). Within each type, there are thousands of 'minutiae' features to be taken into account. For example, ridges in the fingerprint that can end abruptly or divide, or move around other ridges in unusual, notable ways.

In order to speed up the process of comparing fingerprints, prints are now scanned into computers. These computers annotate the minutiae for points of comparison and the results are held in an AFIS database: an Automated Fingerprint Identification System. Countries tend to operate their own AFISs. In America, the FBI owns the Integrated Automated Fingerprint Identification System (IAFIS), into which fingerprint information is voluntarily submitted by state and federal law-enforcement agencies. It is the world's largest biometric database, containing details of over 47 million suspects. CSI

LAS VEGAS METRO POLICE DEPARTMENT

FINGERPRINT MATCH

NAME: PAUL MILLANDER

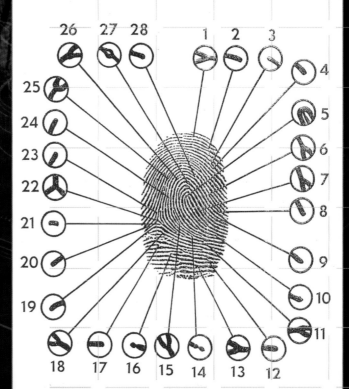

DADDY'S GIRL

Season five's epic two-part finale *Grave Danger* saw guest director Quentin Tarantino mess with the Vegas CSIs' minds. Jailbird Kelly Gordon, played by AIMEE GRAHAM, went along for the thrilling ride...

"**I** would love to go back to *CSI*," says Aimee Graham, the face behind *Grave Danger*'s haunting Kelly Gordon. "I wish they hadn't killed me in season six, but I don't know how they would bring me back unless I was a ghost, or a twin sister nobody knew about."

We tell her that on *CSI* almost anything's possible. And why not? She's one of only a handful of guest stars who the writers brought back a whole season later, to round off her character's harrowing story.

Ask anyone to name their favorite *CSI: Crime Scene Investigation* episodes, and nine times out of 10 season five's finale *Grave Danger* will crop up on the list. Ignore, if you can, the fact the two-parter is helmed by directorial demigod Quentin Tarantino of *Pulp Fiction* fame, and involves one of George Eads' most memorable performances (despite the fact he only has himself for company for the whole two-parter), and focus on the brilliance of the set-up: CSI gets buried alive while his buddies race against the clock to save him. Pure genius! And Graham agrees...

"I generally don't watch myself but I wanted to see how this turned out," Graham explains when we caught up with her recently. "Of course, the finished product is always going to look slightly different from what you imagine, but Quentin did a great job, it's a lot scarier than I thought it would be. And the fact people remember it means it obviously had some impact."

Indeed it did. The shocking suicide of the kidnapper at the end of the first half leaves the CSIs desperately searching for the slowly suffocating Stokes. Their hunt brings them to Kelly, the bad guy's daughter who's in prison for accessory to murder. Suffering terrible abuse at the hands of her fellow inmates, Kelly shows no pity for Nick's situation. Not exactly an easy mind-set to get into for the Wisconsin-born actress.

"I thought about the story a lot and what her life would have been like before this incident occurred and how this one moment had altered her forever," Graham recalls. "I actually read a couple of books about women in prison to prepare for the role, and I thought about her experiences being there. I also thought a lot about the relationship with her dad and how sad it must be for him to see her go through these changes and not be able to do anything about it."

Although Graham was well aware being on *CSI* should be a fun experience, and as much as she wanted to enjoy her time there, she tried to stay focused on the job in hand. "It would have been great to hang out and joke around, but I was pretty focused on what I was doing. I tried to do as much work and research as possible... It's not a great place to be in your mind." And the character's drawn-out look really helped create the character – for Graham as well as for the audience. "I didn't want to wear a lot of make-up," she says. "Quentin went out of his way to make

the episode as gritty as possible. I didn't have much make-up, or get any touch-ups. It's pretty grim being in prison, and I wouldn't have wanted to be made-up and pretty – I hate when shows do that."

Graham, who's had parts in *From Dusk Till Dawn* and *Jackie Brown*, was no stranger to Quentin Tarantino's gritty ways when she took on the role – but what was he like to work with this time around? "It was great!" she enthuses. "It was good to see him again. He's a really great director, and he's really good with the actors. He knows the right things to say and genuinely cares about the characters and the story."

Like Quentin, Graham was just visiting *CSI* and with only a few short but intense scenes, one would assume it would be hard fitting in. "The cast was great, too," she clarifies. "My stuff was mostly with Paul [Guilfoyle], Jorja [Fox], and George [Eads] and they were all very nice and friendly. Of course, you're sort of visiting somebody else's home, but they were all very gracious, and went out of their way to make me feel comfortable."

So comfortable, in fact, that after that final lingering look at the end of season five, a year later Graham was back at *CSI* H.Q. to conclude the story in the season six episode *Daddy's Little Girl*, where Kelly met a miserable end. "To be honest with you, I felt there was some sort of hope for the character at the end of *Grave Danger*," she reveals. "Maybe nobody else saw

"**Que**ntin did a great job, it's a lot scarier than I thought it would be!" >>>>>>

it like that! I didn't know what turn they would take with it. Kelly was a victim of her circumstances, so I'd hoped she would've been able to pull herself out of it and get on with her life. In reality, when you read these stories about women in prison, it's not like they go to jail and people really try to reform them. I'm sure lots of people end up in a similar situation to Kelly."

Kelly's sad demise means it's unlikely Graham will be back on the show, although she does get excited when we suggest she makes a play for the rest of the franchise – "I'd love to do that! Hopefully you'll see me on one of the other *CSIs* soon!" But three years down the line she clearly relishes her *CSI* experience. "It was great material, obviously," she says, "Everybody was so nice – the actors, the crew... I haven't worked on a lot of television, but *CSI* is an interesting show. It's smart, well written, and they get great people to direct on there, too!" csi

>>>>>>>>>>>>>>>>>>>>>>>>>>>>>>> **SEASON** ⟩

IN HER EIGHT YEARS WORKING THE LAS VEGAS GRAVEYARD SHIFT, SARA SIDLE FACED MORE THAN HER FAIR SHARE OF HEARTACHE, WHICH EVENTUALLY RESULTED IN HER LEAVING SIN CITY. ACTRESS JORJA FOX RECALLS HER TIME ON *CSI: CRIME SCENE INVESTIGATION*...

GIRL, INTERRUPTED

When it comes to Sara Sidle, it's definitely a case of gone but not forgotten for the show's millions of fans. And that goes for Jorja Fox too. Several months after bidding *CSI: Crime Scene Investigation* farewell in season 8, the 39-year-old actress explains what attracted her to the character in the first place, and reveals what she misses most about working on the series. She also talks about "that" bedroom scene...

Looking back, what do you recall about landing the plum part of Sara Sidle?
I remember it fairly well actually. I had been working on *The West Wing* at the time. I kept getting phone calls from friends asking, "Hey, have you heard of this show? They are adding this character at the last minute. You should check it out." I was really happy at *The West Wing*. I didn't pursue it at all. I was like, "No thank you, but thanks for thinking of me." Then finally, a script came from my agency and it was the show my friends had been calling me about. Probably five pages in, I fell into a trance, knew I had to go meet everybody, and that

if I was lucky enough that they were going to cast me, I was going to have to take the job. It was this magnetic pull and I couldn't stop it anymore. There was a little byline for the character, Sara Sidle, and it said she was from San Francisco, was just coming in to help on an internal case in Las Vegas, that she was going to be a love interest for Grissom, was really tough, had poor social skills, and could drink anyone under the table. It has been pretty consistently like that for seven years so they were right on. I went in, met everybody for the first time – I had been run over accidentally on *The West Wing* a month or two before so I was limping around. I thought there was no way they were going to hire this actress with these crutches. They brought me back and who knew? I ended up getting it so I was thrilled.

In the beginning, Sara ruffled a few feathers, especially Catherine's. Were you concerned there would be this continuing tension?
They had written some stuff very early in the show for us, and Marg [Helgenberger] and I both sat down together and didn't really want that to happen,

primarily because we were the only two women on the show. We talked about it, then took it to the writers and asked if we could not do that. They could butt heads but we didn't want them intrinsically at odds. The writers were kind enough to amend that.

Sara's past comes back to haunt her when it's revealed that her mother murdered her father and she was then taken into foster care. How did that tragic past shape who Sara was?
Again, that was something the writers had decided early on, that a traumatic event in Sara's past had led her to where she was, led her down this road of working in forensics. Nobody knew what that looked like completely until close to that episode, *Committed*. We talked about it, had thrown ideas around, so I always knew there was something she had, was protecting or hiding, and something that made her job extremely personal for her. That was a wonderful thing to play and it raised the stakes even more. So many people have to work on professional detachment in order to go to work everyday, like firefighters, cops, people who work in emergency rooms, and obviously crime scene investigators.

In *Bloodlines*, Sara was picked up for a DUI. Did that make sense to you?
Like many of the personal storylines for Sara, that came completely out of left field. Surprise. There was a little internal struggle for me because there was a part of me that didn't want that to happen to Sara. I am very protective of her so I felt that would never happen, that it was terrible, and this is Vegas where you can take a cab. I didn't want her to be seen as that vulnerable and yet at the same time, I did believe it could happen to her. It is a really human thing and nothing anyone is proud of. It is a moment in a person's life where they take a fall. Looking back on that tiny little character breakdown from season one, it was very much in line with something that could happen to

her, although at the end of the day, I do think she is slightly smarter than that.

How was it having the CSI team spilt into the day shift and night shift?
For the writers, going into that season, it was obviously something they could do that would be different and interesting. How would the dynamics develop between all the characters? On a personal level, I was just sad I wasn't going to see George [Eads], Gary [Dourdan], and Marg a lot that season. I love working with everyone and there is no scene partner I don't adore, so I was bummed.

During that period, Sara took Greg under her wing and they seemed to develop a strong bond. Was there a romance brewing between the two investigators?
There is always a possibility of a relationship there. Greg is Sara's best friend outside of Grissom but he was probably too young for her. I think she saw him much more as a little brother or friend. It has been awesome watching Eric Szmanda, who is the youngest guy on the show, and outside of work is one of my best friends, go from 24 to 33. Many, many moons later, if things really fell apart between Grissom and Sara, I do wonder if there would be a time for Greg and Sara. I think Greg is completely over Sara but she still holds a certain torch for him.

Originally, Sara was supposed to be a love interest for Grissom but they only seemed to commit to that recently. Did all that speculation and dancing around ever get frustrating?
No, not at all. That is one of the cool things about getting to do something over a long period of time. When they decided to bring it back, I had almost decided the audience was sick of the idea of Sara and Grissom. There had been this weird dance that had played out over a couple of seasons that had really led nowhere it seemed. For Billy [Petersen] and I as actors, coming into season one, because it was on the page, we started the show playing it. It was the producers' decision to pull back on it. There is some truth to the idea that when they realized the show might be on the air for a while,

"The seven years of William Petersen, Eric Szmanda, George Eads, Gary, Marg, David Hall, Paul, and Wally. That's the thing I will cherish the most!"

WHO ARE YOU?

SARA SIDLE PROFILE

CSI Sara Sidle has always led an eventful life. She first appeared on CSI as a replacement for rookie Holly Gribbs, who was murdered in *Pilot* (1.01), at which point Grissom was already referring to her as "a friend". It would take six seasons for their friendship to blossom into the relationship Sara seemed to long for – and just one more for crazed 'Miniature Killer' Natalie Davis to use this as a reason to target her. (She had another 'office romance' during that time, with assistant paramedic Hank Pettigrew; they split because he cheated on her.)

Born to hippy parents living outside San Francisco, Sara was taken into foster care after her mother stabbed her violent, alcoholic father to death and was institutionalized – as a result, Sara often identifies with victims of abuse. Despite her disruptive home life, she excelled academically and graduated from Harvard and Berkeley before training as a CSI in San Francisco, where she met Grissom at an entomology lecture. An intense CSI, she's not always able to detach her emotions from her job – in *Bloodlines* (4.23), when Nick wins a promotion instead of her, Sara drowns her sorrows and is caught drunk driving; Grissom collects her from the station. When she's suspended in *Nesting Dolls* (5.13) after rowing with Catherine then Ecklie over another domestic abuse case, Grissom visits her at home for an explanation. Telling her alcohol isn't her problem, he asks why she's angry and Sara tells him about the night her mother killed her father. Their subsequent relationship gave her the comfort and security she lacked and craved – but ultimately it wasn't enough to keep her in Las Vegas, and she apparently left the City Of Sin for good in *Goodbye And Good Luck* (8.07).

slightly alienated and lonely by nature of what they do. To know there is this little light burning somewhere in their lives was amazing payback and what Sara and Grissom really deserve.

What was your take on doing an ongoing arc like the Miniature Killer storyline?
I loved the fact that we were going to take on a story that would go the whole season. I wasn't thrilled with the idea of becoming a victim of the serial killer though. Maybe I wasn't completely listening because Carol and Ann did mention something to me about how this thing would go all season, that there would be something between Sara and the serial killer, but when push came to shove, I wasn't really for that at all. I was extremely protective of the character. I felt Sara had been victimized as a child, had gone through so much, and had made such a heroic stand at not being a victim anymore, which is partly how she ended up at the crime labs. But it makes excellent drama and speaking of the season eight premiere, it was fun to shoot it. I am really glad I did it and have no regrets.

The eighth season premiere, *Dead Doll*, had Sara in pretty dire circumstances. How was it filming that wet, deadly trap?
There was a lot of water involved. I am a bit claustrophobic and I've also been hurt a couple of times doing stunts so I'm pretty much the wimp of the cast. I'm the last one in line to do anything dangerous and would much rather sit in the lab with a microscope. Again, I was like, "Why me? Please. Eric, George, and Gary love to do that!" I had a few things working against me in terms of the physicality of the stuff. The cool thing about water and me is that I'm an avid surfer and I love water. The water stuff is fun; it was the two tons of steel hanging over my head that gave me the creeps.

When rumors started circulating that you could be the killer's next victim, there was a 'Save Sara' campaign. It must be very gratifying to know your fans are so loyal.
It is amazing to me that after seven years people would still be invested enough to take the time to actually write those letters or send those emails. It is almost intangibly flattering. It is hard to communicate how meaningful that is. If you don't mind printing just a huge "Thank you" and "I love you" to the people who have been kind enough to check out what I am doing – I am sure it is the reason I am still doing it.

There have been so many bloody and gory episodes. Is there one that really disturbed you?
If I was speaking personally about going too far, I'd say most of them. I am so squeamish. I am a pacifist

SARA SIDLE'S SCREEN CREDITS

Big fan of Jorja Fox? Then make sure you check out...

The West Wing (2000)
– as Agent Gina Toscano
Starring in six episodes, Jorja plays the security detail to First Daughter Zoey Bartlet.

Memento (2000)
– as Leonard's Wife
Jorja plays Guy Pearce's deceased wife in this beautifully crafted thriller from *Batman Begins* director Christopher Nolan.

E.R. (1999)
– as Dr. Maggie Doyle
As the no-nonsense Dr. Maggie Doyle, Jorja certainly made her mark on this long-running medical drama, with her character suing the hospital.

Velocity Trap (1997)
– as Alice Pallas
Set in the distant future, a team of mercenaries plot to hijack an armored ship carrying millions of dollars. Jorja plays one of the sharpshooters.

they didn't want to play all their cards in the first couple of seasons. For me, there is a wonderful feeling that viewers still want to know more about those characters.

Things finally heated up in the sixth season finale when Sara strolled out in a bathrobe...
That was interesting because there was a different ending planned for the show, a cliffhanger, and we had already started shooting the episode. I got a phone call in the afternoon from Carol Mendelsohn and Ann Donahue together and they were like, "What do you think about this?" That's another great thing about working on *CSI* – the writers will actually call you up and ask you what you think about a storyline. They were definitely giving me the option to say I didn't want to do it. So I was completely surprised and quickly said, "Yeah!" It was very last minute and I thought it was an amazing Grissom scene. We rarely hear his innermost feelings. The show is so dark and the characters are so driven, they all seem

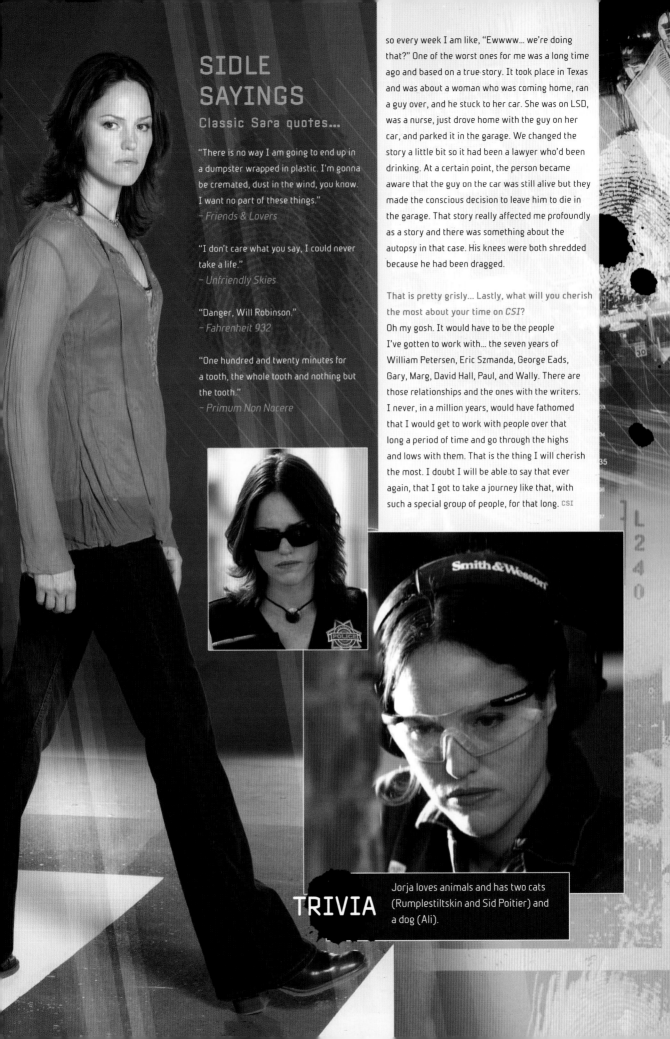

SIDLE SAYINGS
Classic Sara quotes...

"There is no way I am going to end up in a dumpster wrapped in plastic. I'm gonna be cremated, dust in the wind, you know. I want no part of these things."
– *Friends & Lovers*

"I don't care what you say, I could never take a life."
– *Unfriendly Skies*

"Danger, Will Robinson."
– *Fahrenheit 932*

"One hundred and twenty minutes for a tooth, the whole tooth and nothing but the tooth."
– *Primum Non Nocere*

so every week I am like, "Ewwww... we're doing that?" One of the worst ones for me was a long time ago and based on a true story. It took place in Texas and was about a woman who was coming home, ran a guy over, and he stuck to her car. She was on LSD, was a nurse, just drove home with the guy on her car, and parked it in the garage. We changed the story a little bit so it had been a lawyer who'd been drinking. At a certain point, the person became aware that the guy on the car was still alive but they made the conscious decision to leave him to die in the garage. That story really affected me profoundly as a story and there was something about the autopsy in that case. His knees were both shredded because he had been dragged.

That is pretty grisly... Lastly, what will you cherish the most about your time on *CSI*?
Oh my gosh. It would have to be the people I've gotten to work with... the seven years of William Petersen, Eric Szmanda, George Eads, Gary, Marg, David Hall, Paul, and Wally. There are those relationships and the ones with the writers. I never, in a million years, would have fathomed that I would get to work with people over that long a period of time and go through the highs and lows with them. That is the thing I will cherish the most. I doubt I will be able to say that ever again, that I got to take a journey like that, with such a special group of people, for that long. CSI

TRIVIA
Jorja loves animals and has two cats (Rumplestiltskin and Sid Poitier) and a dog (Ali).

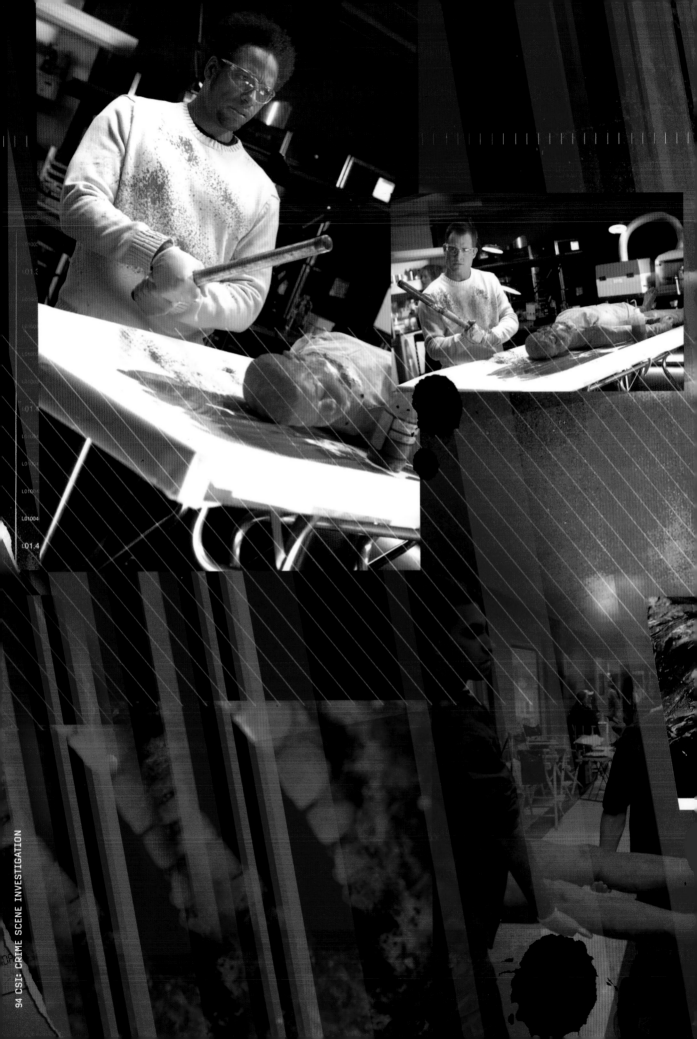

HOUSE OF HORRORS

Where do the producers of CSI: Crime Scene Investigation go when they need a decaying body, a hairy werewolf lady or a removable brain? To Oscar-winning special effects make-up expert Matthew W. Mungle...

Matthew W. Mungle

Walking into Matthew W. Mungle's production facility, located on a nondescript street in L.A.'s North Hollywood district, you wouldn't expect to be stepping into movie history. But such is Mungle's career that it's impossible to avoid – posters from his lengthy, Oscar-winning career as a special effects make-up artist and prop creator adorn the walls of the reception area. Everything from classics such as *Schindler's List* and *Jurassic Park* to more recent jobs like creating Katherine Heigl's pregnant belly for the comedy *Knocked Up*. And when he takes you on into the main workshop floor, there's another treat lurking – the walls here are lined with head casts of all the stars who've been here to have make-up effects created: Leonardo DiCaprio shares space with Robin Williams. It's like a scene from *Futurama*...

Given his reputation, our first question has long since gone out of the window. He didn't need to push for the job, the *CSI* team came to him just before the fifth season of the show. "They were searching for a new company to do the make-up effects," Mungle recalls. Plus, it wasn't like he was a stranger to the franchise... "We had already done the first season and a half of *CSI: Miami*, so we'd gotten into the loop. Then *Miami* started cutting their 'gross factor' back a little bit so we weren't needed on that show. There was a lag of about a year before the original *CSI* team came to us and wanted to know if we'd do the show, and I was more than willing. They had been doing it for four years and knew exactly what they were up to. Everyone is so nice and so easygoing. They came to us and were very impressed with our lab and all of our research, so we got the job!"

So what exactly does the job entail? Roughly speaking, Mungle's effects team is called upon to handle all the dead bodies and other complicated make-up effects seen on the show. Whenever Robert David Hall's Doc Robbins is slicing into a corpse, or William Petersen's Grissom inspects a crime scene, you'll see his work on screen. But, of course, the trip from script to screen behind the scenes is a little more complicated.

"We'll get a script, probably about five days before shooting and then if there's a full body in there, I'll talk with the assistant director and make sure they can push that towards the end of the schedule. Most of the time they can, but sometimes there's a time crunch with actors or locations and so it doesn't always work out. Either way, we just have to get it done. If it's a really big episode and they know we'll have to do quite a bit of prep work, they'll let us know two episodes ahead of time that they'll need something or give us a writer's draft of the script, but that's very rare. We'll break it down, I'll go and have a meeting with the director about what he wants to see – sometimes I talk to the producer before the director's even hired – to pick his brain about what we need to do. Once I've had that meeting, we go full steam ahead on it."

TRIVIA: Matthew W. Mungle estimates that his make-up and props department get through 30 gallons of fake plasma a season on CSI alone.

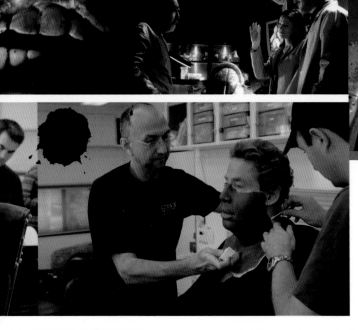

"I love my job because it's so fast and you're always thinking on your feet."

ALL SHAPES AND SIZES

The fast turnaround at *CSI* means that Mungle and his team have to work fast, whether they're creating a dead body, turning one of the guest actors into a corpse or creating a specific make-up look. "We do a show in eight days of shooting and then there's an extra day for inserts and one for 'CSI shots'."

Ah yes, one of *CSI*'s signatures, and one much aped by other shows – a quick trip around the heart or a shot of a bullet entering someone's chest – are created using a blend of Mungle's specially-built practical pieces and computer trickery. "Lately they've been doing a little more CGI for that – flying through bullet holes and so on – and fewer practical effects. Sometimes we'll give them the practical and they'll use it. But then they'll use CG to augment it."

The process involves using latex prosthetics to either sculpt a piece to fit an actor or, in the case of those dying for their art, a full head cast that will eventually end up atop one of Mungle's stock bodies (latex molded pieces that come in a variety of shapes and sizes). "We can use different heads because most of the time it's either make-up on an actor or a fake body," Mungle explains. "If it's a fake body that has

to look like a certain actor, they'll send the actor in as soon as possible, as soon as they have the role. We'll cast their head, make a mold of that and find a stock body that matches their body type and then put their head onto that body."

Not all dead bodies are created equally, of course – some are more of a challenge than others. "There was one episode that we did called *Big Middle*, in season five, and it was a deteriorating body over time. It was done in the teaser. You saw the sun coming up, going down, the moon rising and you saw all the body gasses growing in the body and a wolf coming and eating it, and it deteriorating and the maggots feeding on it. That was intense to do and a fun one. Another one was an episode where we had to show

the decay of a body that had been encapsulated in tar (*Nesting Dolls*). We had to show the skin melting off the body, so we did it with old-fashioned gelatin and hot lamps. That was very cool."

Yes, this is a man who truly loves his work. Even if sometimes it makes his collaborators feel a little sickly. "Last year I did an episode called *Fannysmackin'* with director Richard J. Lewis. They had to remove some guy's brain, so I said, 'Let's pull the whole skin down over his eyes, so you see his eyes outside of the skin.' It became more of a cartoony-looking thing, even though that's realistically what would have happened, that just became pretty darn gross and he's since shied away from things that we've done. I ribbed him for ages about that: 'Well, you asked for it...'"

Naturally, what you can and can't show on television is a big consideration for Mungle. But he's protected by both his own knowledge of what will not make the final version and the producers' dealings with network TV's Standards & Practices department, which gives notes on everything from swearing to death. "I keep that in mind because we can do whatever we want to do, but they'd end up cutting it back, so we cut ourselves back anyway and keep it from the cutting room floor. And they know how much they can get away with and how much they can't, so they give us those parameters. They check with the network before we get our shooting draft of the script. Most of the time we get three or four drafts of the script before we get the final shooting version." And he's also ready for the advances in TV technology, with HD screens meaning viewers get a much clearer look at his work. It's not really a problem for someone used to having his effects up on the big screen, however. "We've always done it to that level and I never tend to worry. We try to bring that technology from the movies into TV, which is good for them because they get the benefit of our experience."

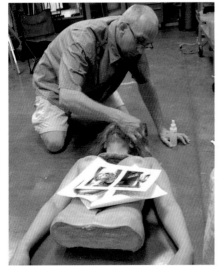

It's not all creating dead people and helping make realistic autopsy scenes – Mungle has been called upon for a few other memorable moments. "In my four years of working on this show, I've had one test on a make-up. And that was because I requested it. That was the werewolf episode with the hair on the face – because there are so many ways that can go bad. We got the actress three days before and did a test on her with all the hair and it worked fine."

But there was another challenge – when the character's dead brother needed more than the usual autopsy attention. "He had to lay there and they had to shave him on set. We had to shave his hair off or show like we were, take him back to the trailer, take all the hair off, paint stubble over his body and send him back to the set so they could shoot him after the fact. So they really had to work that out in the schedule."

When prompted to recall another memorable job, Mungle picks one out easily. "One of my particular favourites was *Living Legend* from last season, with Roger Daltrey, where we did four different disguises on him. We had plenty of set up on that. In fact, executive producer Carol Mendelsohn, for the first episode of season seven said, 'Have I got an episode for you...' And I asked, 'What is it?' And she said, 'It's kind of like *The List Of Adrian Messenger* where someone dresses up and pulls off all the disguises.' So we made sure I had at least two months prep on that. We got Roger when he wasn't on his tour (with The Who) to go into a friend's at the special effects company Animated Extras to get his face cast so I could start the process. That was a fun episode."

RESEARCH, RESEARCH, RESEARCH

With so much experience handling the dead bodies of *CSI*, you have to wonder if Mungle and his artists spend a lot of time hanging around in morgues to gather their research. But their sources are a lot easier – and less smelly – to deal with. "We've got tonnes of forensics books that we can go to and also there's a great autopsy book called *Color Atlas Of The Autopsy*, and it shows one being done from beginning to end. It shows all the organs and how they look, and that's what we try to reproduce. Plus, sometimes we go online. It's amazing what you can find these days."

It might seem strange that a man more used to working for mega-budget Hollywood productions like the films of Steven Spielberg would want to tackle the high-speed, lower-budget world of TV, but Mungle – whose facility handles the prosthetics work for the likes of *NCIS*, *House* and even *Desperate Housewives*, while still keeping up a healthy film career (such as a little film called *Indiana Jones and the Kingdom of the Crystal Skull*) – cheerfully admits that he relishes the added pressure.

"I love it, because it's so fast and you're always thinking on your feet. Sometimes it's a case of, 'Well, we can't do this, which would take four days to do, so let's do this, which will only take two days.' It is a challenge, but we rise to the challenge." CSI

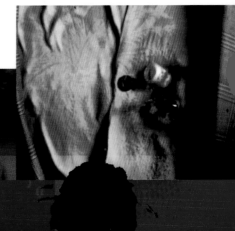

CSI: DEAD DOLL
SARA PINNED SEQUENCE
Director: Ken Fink
Storyboard: Brian Murray
07.18.07

CLASSIC
STORYBOARD
#1

SURVIVAL INSTINCT

Over the summer of 2007, there was only one question on the lips of *CSI: Crime Scene Investigation* fans: Would Sara survive? Thankfully the answer was yes, but it was a close run thing, with Sara's sheer determination and a huge stroke of luck making the only difference between her living and dying. Now we've gained access to the storyboards used by the production team to visualize her dramatic escape, courtesy of *CSI* artist Brian Murray...

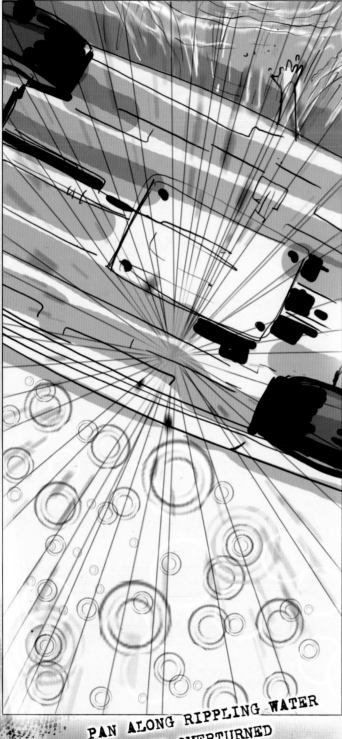

PAN ALONG RIPPLING WATER
AND OVER OVERTURNED
CAR TO FIND SARA'S HAND

SARA'S POINT OF VIEW OF
WATER RUSHING TOWARD HER.

REVERSE ON SARA IN DISTRESS.

PINNED UNDER THE CAR.
AS WATER RISES AROUND HER...

...SHE DUCKS UNDER THE SURFACE...

TO FIND HER ARM FIRMLY WEDGED
BETWEEN THE CAR AND THE GROUND.

TRIVIA

The season eight premiere *Dead Doll* took 10 days to film (two more than normal), with the 'Sara Pinned' sequence taking a day-and-a-half.

SHE BURSTS THROUGH THE SURFACE FOR SOME AIR

SHE GOES BACK UNDER

LOOKING FOR ANYTHING TO HELP

HER POINT OF VIEW ON THE CAR RESTING ON ROCKS AND MUD

UP AGAIN FOR ANOTHER GULP OF AIR...

TRIVIA

The crew built a mock-up of the desert scene on a Californian soundstage, which included a car on hydraulics. They used it to film all the close-up shots.

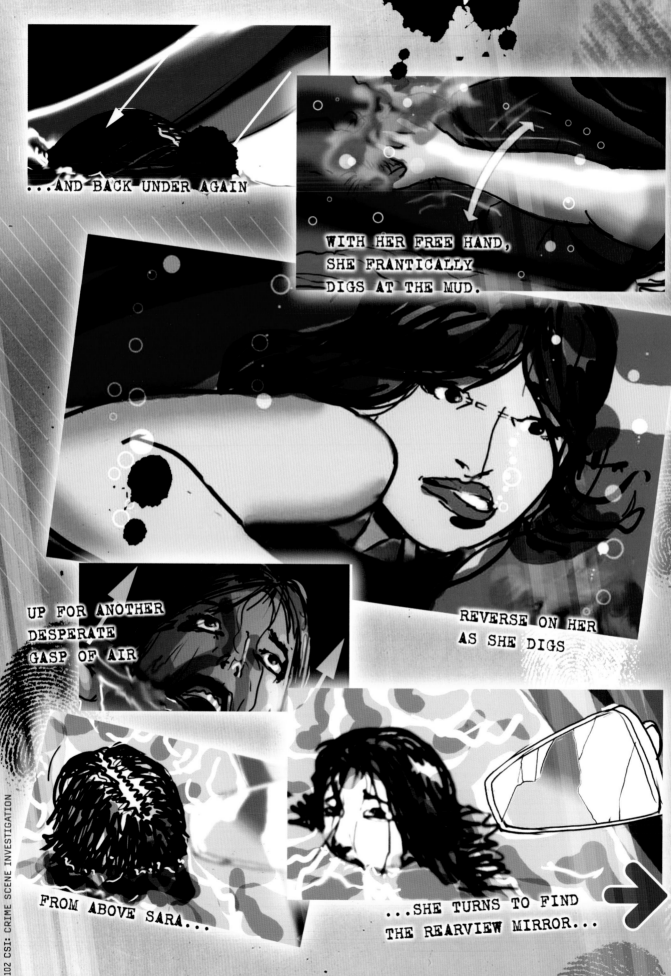

...AND BACK UNDER AGAIN

WITH HER FREE HAND, SHE FRANTICALLY DIGS AT THE MUD.

UP FOR ANOTHER DESPERATE GASP OF AIR

REVERSE ON HER AS SHE DIGS

FROM ABOVE SARA...

...SHE TURNS TO FIND THE REARVIEW MIRROR...

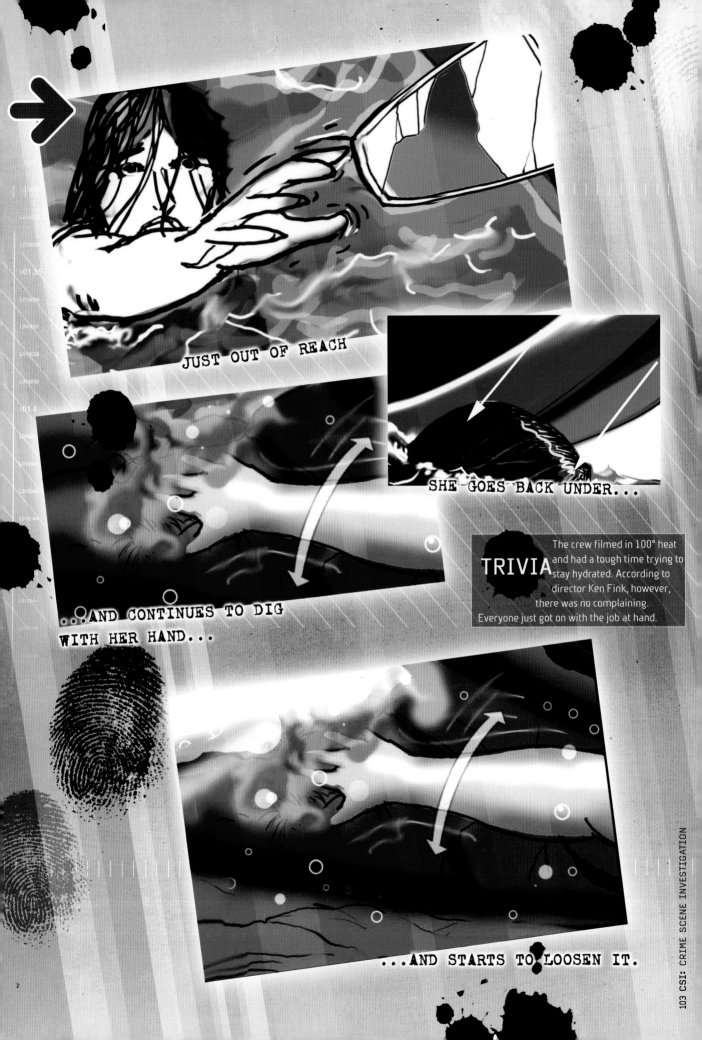

JUST OUT OF REACH

SHE GOES BACK UNDER...

...AND CONTINUES TO DIG
WITH HER HAND...

TRIVIA The crew filmed in 100° heat and had a tough time trying to stay hydrated. According to director Ken Fink, however, there was no complaining. Everyone just got on with the job at hand.

...AND STARTS TO LOOSEN IT.

FROM THE OPPOSITE SIDE OF THE ROCKS AND MUD ON HER HAND DIGGING THROUGH...

AND THE SUPPORT ROCK TUMBLING. FOLLOWED BY THE CAR TEETERING.

CLOSE AS SHE BREAKS THE SURFACE.

BACK ON HER POINT OF VIEW FOR THE CAR TEETERING.

WIDER AS SHE MOVES OUT OF THE WATER BENEATH...

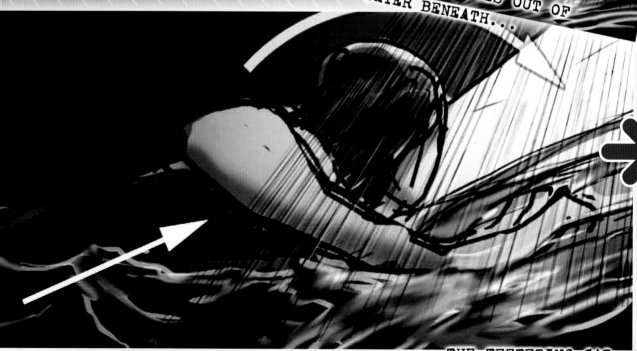

...THE TEETERING CAR.

CLOSE UP ON HER FURY
AS SHE WALKS OUT OF THE WATER...

CONTINUE TO
PULL OUT
AS THE CAR...

SMASHES DOWN, CRUSHING THE SPOT
SHE WAS JUST IN, AS SHE CONTINUES
PAST CAMERA.

INNOCENCE LOST

JULIETTE GOGLIA EPISODES
Goodbye And Good Luck
(8.07)
The Unusual Suspect
(6.18)

Before The Miniature Killer set her sights on Sara, she was taken for a ride by an altogether different sort of miniature killer – a 12-year-old girl named Hannah West. JULIETTE GOGLIA talks exclusively about being the youngest criminal on the block in season six's brilliant *The Unusual Suspect*.

Hannah West was a very dark, complex character. How do you prepare for something like that?
After I read the script, I thought that Hannah was really brilliant, cunning, and motivated by an intense love for her brother. After that, I played off of Jorja Fox on set, and she really helped me become Hannah, in the moment, and that's how I got most of my inspiration for that role. Jorja Fox has always been a huge role model for me because she's such a brilliant actress – the way that she approaches her roles is so convincing. On set we were always having fun, and she was just such a joy to be around. I want to work with her a ton more in the future!

What was it like walking on to the *CSI* set for the first time?
It was a little intimidating, but actually really exciting! Auditions for the part of Hannah had been really intense, so I was thrilled to find out I had got the part! It's such a big show and being on set was just a confirmation, and very emotional for me. I was really excited! The set isn't crazy and uptight but it was very serious – it's a drama and you have to be very focused. I really enjoyed working with the crew and the cast and everyone.

How did you feel about playing a possibly murderous character?
I was really excited, because usually the parts for a 12-year-old girl are your typically bratty teenager. But when I read the breakdown for this dark and complex character I was thrilled, and jumped at the opportunity! It was one of my dream roles, to play a little, dark murderer! It's been my favorite part to play by far.

You first played Hannah a couple of years ago, when you were just 11. Were you able to watch *CSI* before you got the part?
Well, my parents are really overprotective! It's a gory show and it can be inappropriate at times, so I was not allowed to watch the show. I still, to this day, have not seen the first full episode that I did, because there were some inappropriate scenes. I saw my scenes of course!

Did coming to the show fresh make it harder to prepare for the role?
I don't think that it necessarily made it harder because I hadn't watched the show. My mom watches the show and she gave me enough background info. I also knew the network, and the season that they were on, so I could get a vibe of how the actors worked.

Being a younger actress, could you relate to Hannah's experience as a fast-tracked student?
I could really relate to Hannah in that sense. Personally, I've always been more comfortable around adults than kids my own age because, when you're around adults, you have to be able to keep up with the conversation and be sophisticated. I'm usually surrounded by adults, so I've had a lot of experience in that field. I enjoyed it, and definitely related to how Hannah had to really step up her game and be just as smart, or smarter than the adults in that situation.

Hannah definitely got under Sara's skin. Why do you think she resonated with Sara?
I think that Sara was first drawn to Hannah because she thought that she could help her. I know that Sara, as a teenager, was exceedingly smart; and I know that in some ways she saw Hannah as a younger version of herself. When Hannah was doing all these horrible things – whether she murdered the girl or not – Sara wanted to help her. I think it was also really irritating for her because Hannah was the first person who had tricked her, and made her think the opposite of what really happened. I think that pushed her buttons, and she was a little taken aback. I was pretty amazed to know that Hannah had such an effect on Sara, but I actually felt a little bad that Hannah might be one of the reasons for Sara's leaving. CSI

"I still, to this day, have not seen the first full episode that I did, because ther

Б

In celebration of Jorja Fox's time on CSI: Crime Scene Investigation, we [...] back at Sara Sidle's 10 most memorable moments...

THE SIDLE COUNTDO[...]

WOULD YOU LIKE FLIES WITH THAT?
– Sara Becomes A Vegetarian

When? *Sex, Lies And Larvae*, season 1, episode 10

What? As a top CSI, Sara's a pretty tough cookie, but this episode proves that some cases do take their toll on a CSI's private life – and their stomach! A bug-ridden, rotting body is found, and though Grissom is in his element, Sara finds the scene most off-putting. Their initial evidence doesn't carry enough weight for a conviction, but Sara just can't let go of the case. She tells Grissom she has nightmares and hears the victim's screams. The two of them carry out further decomposition tests with pig flesh and flies – gross! It is revealed in a later episode that Sara had more than enough pork in this case and couldn't face eating meat again afterwards. Perfectly understandable we think!

"I never get used to this part, you know, when the flies get going."

FIRST IMPRESSIONS
– Sara's Arrival

When? *Cool Change*, season 1, episode 2

What? Even before we meet Sara Sidle, it's clear that she and Grissom already know each other well. But, of course, nothing is given away about the exact nature of their relationship. Despite being personally called to Vegas by Grissom, Sara dismisses any sense of intimacy or nostalgia, instead focusing on the job she's been called in to do. Later, when faced with Catherine's cool reception and hostility, Sara again shows that she has no time for pettiness or personal issues. In what will prove to be true Sidle style, Sara just wants to get down to solving the case.

"Look, we could stand here and argue, or we could get out there and find who did this... Two sharp women are better than one."

JUST CAN'T BREAK AWAY
– Sara Loses Her Cool

When? *Too Tough To Die*, season 1, episode 15

What? Here we see Sara's tendency to get emotionally involved in cases due to their subject matter, as well as her lack of social life. Having to carry out tests on a victim who is still alive, Sara finds it hard not to personalize the situation. She talks to the victim and builds up a kind of relationship with her, even though she is lying in a vegetative state. Grissom highlights Sara's deep involvement and discovers she has no outside interests to escape from work. Quite rightly, he is concerned and urges her to detach herself from her cases. Already distressed, Sara finds this advice unwelcome.

"I wish I was like you Grissom, I wish I didn't feel anything."

A CRASH COURSE IN LOVE
– Sara Discovers Her Boyfriend Is Two-Timing Her

When? *Crash And Burn*, season 3, episode 17

What? Sara's professional and private lives collide when her boyfriend is involved in a crash she investigates. We see a softer side to her and it is almost surprising to find her distracted from work when she concentrates on him, and even pauses her questioning to talk to him. But things don't run smoothly as Sara discovers this man, who has clearly had a significant impact on her, is in a long-term relationship with another woman. Sara is stunned but doesn't cause a scene. Even when the pair say their goodbyes, there are no tears, no hysterics from Sara, just a sad sense of loss and disappointment.

"You never know when your life's going to change."

A RISK WORTH TAKING?
– Sara Asks Grissom Out

When? *Play With Fire*, season 3, episode 22

What? Sara has a few risky moments in this episode, culminating in possibly the biggest risk a girl can take – asking a guy out! Knocked down in a lab explosion, she is lucky to walk away without major injury. Getting straight back to work, however, sees her entering a gang member's home before it has been cleared by the cops. After these close encounters, Sara takes the plunge and asks Grissom out. But what does he say? No! Though he does admit there is something between them, this is obviously not the outcome she was hoping for. Her closing words show her hurt and leave us wondering what will become of their relationship.

"You know, by the time you figure it out, it really could be too late."

GROWING PAINS
– Sara And Catherine Bust Up

When? *Nesting Dolls*, season 5, episode 13

What? In a suspected domestic violence case, Sara, as we've seen before, becomes over-involved and crosses the line with the suspect. When Catherine pulls her up on this, Sara again gets personal and insults her. She just doesn't know when to stop and following a further confrontation with Ecklie, Sara is suspended. In a moving, intimate scene, Grissom forces Sara to open up about why she is so angry. Her behavior is explained as we learn that she grew up in an abusive family. Painfully, she shares with Grissom her memories of the traumatic night she was taken into foster care when her mother stabbed her father to death.

"The fights, the yelling, the trips to the hospital. I thought it was the way that everybody lived. When my mother killed my father I found out that it wasn't."

A WORKING RELATIONSHIP
– Sara And Grissom Bedroom Scene

When? *Way To Go*, season 6, episode 24

What? It's the moment we'd been waiting for! At last, after six years of wishing and hoping, we see that Sara and Grissom really are more than just colleagues. Throughout the investigation of a corset-wearing civil war enthusiast(!), the couple have several playful scenes, notably pacing out a duel with cameras for guns. But the main concern of the CSIs is Detective Brass, suffering a critical gunshot wound. After a gruelling day, we see Grissom in bed talking intimately to someone about his thoughts on death. It's a real treat as the mystery companion is revealed to be none other than Sara.

"I'm not ready to say goodbye."

A BAD TRIP
– Sara Trapped Under The Car

When? Dead Doll, season 8, episode 1

What? In this dramatic episode, Sara's survival instincts are pushed to the limits. It's a race against time – and the elements – as the team work to rescue her from the Miniature Killer. Things don't look good with Sara trapped under a car and flash flood water rapidly rising. Miraculously, Sara breaks free. But she is not out of danger yet. Injured, dehydrated and disoriented she battles to stay conscious. She talks to herself and even recites her multiplication tables to keep focused. But her body can only take so much. Finally, Nick finds her, collapsed and unconscious. A very relieved Grissom holds her hand as she is airlifted to hospital, and, in a semi-conscious state, Sara sees him looking down at her.

"Just keep going. Don't stop. Three times four is 12."

HONEY, BE MINE?
– Grissom Asks Sara To Marry Him

When? The Case Of The Cross-Dressing Carp, season 8, episode 4

What? It's another rare piece of happiness for Sara and Grissom – and us – to enjoy together. Away from the stress and pressure of the lab, the pair share a precious moment out in the sun by the bee hives. While Sara is proving her trust in Grissom by removing her glove and allowing a bee to settle on her hand, he takes her by surprise and, without ceremony or fuss, suggests that they get married! The occasion is disturbed slightly as Sara's shock results in a bee sting, but her acceptance is a soothing remedy. The proposal is sweetly rounded off as the couple attempt to kiss but can only touch masks in their protective gear!

"Yes. Let's do it."

LEAVING LAS VEGAS
– Sara Leaves Las Vegas

When? Goodbye And Good Luck, season 8, episode 7

What? We see a sad, exhausted Sara in this episode. The strain of thousands of traumatic cases and times when victims couldn't be saved has pushed her to the point where she can take no more. It's a poignant scene as Sara removes her nametag and prepares to leave the locker room for the last time. The sadness deepens as we see Sara riding away in a cab and her voiceover reads her leaving note to Grissom. She tenderly explains how she loves him but has to leave to finally free herself from the troubles of her past. Goodbye and good luck Sara, we'll miss you!

"No matter how hard I try to fight it off, I'm left feeling that I have to go. I have no idea where I'm going, but I know I have to do this. If I don't, I'll self-destruct, and worse, you'll be there to see it happen."

UNTIL RECENTLY NOTHING SEEMED TO BOTHER ROOKIE CSI GREG SANDERS. THEN HE FOUND HIMSELF IN THE WRONG PLACE AT THE WRONG TIME AND HAS SINCE STRUGGLED TO REGAIN HIS JOIE DE VIVRE. ACTOR ERIC SZMANDA RECALLS HOW BOY MET WORLD...

GROWING PAINS

W hen Greg Sanders was promoted from lab tech to CSI Level One, the world seemed to be his oyster. But impressing Gil Grissom isn't easy and for the first few months at least, the flamboyant Greg struggled to find his footing. Having finally proved a valued member of Grissom's team, the young CSI then paid the price for coming to the aid of a local man, who was being badly beaten by a gang of thugs, landing himself in hospital – and court – in the process. In an exclusive interview with *The Official CSI Magazine*, Eric Szmanda ponders all this and much, much more...

When did you get bitten by the acting bug?
I knew from as young as I can remember that I wanted to be an actor. During family gatherings, I would make all my cousins get together to do a performance for my aunts and uncles. Eventually, I was encouraged to join a community theater in the small town where I grew up. One of the first plays I did was *Cabaret*. It was a small part where I sang one song but I knew I liked being in front of an audience, which led to high school stuff. I then got an agent when I was 15 and started auditioning for commercials.

It must have been a culture shock relocating from Wisconsin to Los Angeles.
Yeah, it was. I graduated from high school and I was accepted to an acting school in New York, but my parents weren't supportive of me going from a small

town in Wisconsin to the big city of New York. We had friends and family in Los Angeles so it put their minds at ease that I had someone to call if anything should go wrong. I moved to Pasadena to go to the American Academy of Dramatic Arts. It was fairly suburban compared to Hollywood, so it was a nice transition for me. Obviously, I enjoyed being in school and around a lot of people but it was absolutely a shock. Where I grew up, there wasn't much diversity in terms of ethnicity. I was in a school meeting people from all over the world. I knew I had been sheltered when I was younger so I was really excited to see what else was out there.

Was it a challenge ditching the Wisconsin accent?
Part of the program at the Academy was a speech clinic. No matter where you were from, the instructors would help you speak with more of a standard American speech. I never realized until I was in that school that I even had an accent. I think most people from the Midwest would agree that is a detectable accent but as I've learned from being out here, it is very obvious. I've been out here for 12 years now so it faded away in my day to day speech but whenever I go back home to visit, it comes back right away.

Your big break was an ongoing role in *The Net*. What did you learn from that television series?
For all intents and purposes, *The Net* was my first television gig. I had a couple of small guest

spots but it wasn't extremely demanding. Being a series regular on a show, I realized the responsibilities and the amount of professionalism required to keep a show going. One of the advantages to working on *The Net* was it was filmed in Vancouver so I was removed from the whole Hollywood structure. We didn't have tons of agents and executives from the network coming down. It felt like we were off doing our own project. It was a nice way to ease into things because on my first day of work, I didn't know what hitting your mark meant or finding your light. I hadn't worked on a single camera format like that so it was a big eye opening experience but I had half of a season on that show to learn the ropes. It definitely prepared me for my next job, which was a pilot in which I was the central character.

How did you become involved in *CSI*?

The pilot I was referring to was cast by a casting director named April Webster and her partner Liz Greenberg. They fought really hard for me to get this part in the pilot because there were some executives who wanted someone else. They were strong supporters of mine so when the pilot didn't work out, they kind of felt sorry for me and called me in for this new pilot they were casting called *CSI*. At

TRIVIA

Eric loves dogs and has a golden retriever named Dax.

"Grissom sees a little bit of himself in Greg. Both of us tend to think outside of the box..."

the time, the role was only recurring and totally not me at all. If I remember correctly, it was for someone in their thirties, like a former construction worker who is now a DNA analyst. At the time, I was in my early twenties and I didn't think I would fit that role at all, so I initially passed on it. They called my agent back and said, "No, we really want Eric to come in and be himself, to do what he does and not to try to fulfill any description that has already been laid out there." I went in, did my own thing, the audition was taped by Liz, and then sent to the directors and producers. I recurred on *CSI* for about 13 episodes before I became a series regular.

How does one go from being a recurring character to a full-time role?

It took a while for that offer to come. It was tough being part of a show that was a huge hit and not having any job security or commitment. When I started getting offers to do other shows and *CSI* was doing well, the network and producers decided they wanted to keep everything intact and

not change anything. For fear of losing me to someone else, they offered me the regular role and welcomed me as part of the cast.

Did you have to do any specific preparation to play Greg Sanders?

A lot of research is done on the spot. Where else would you go to do DNA research but a lab, and we have a real lab on set. We have real CSIs that guide us through procedures and make sure we are doing everything according to protocol. It has been a crash course in forensic science for me and I am still learning every time I go to work. Over the years, we've had the opportunity to meet a lot of people that work in the field, and we hear stories from them and get a true perspective.

Right in the beginning, it was obvious Greg had a huge crush on Catherine. How did that start and was it fun to play?

I remember the first time that really came out was in an episode where Catherine and Greg

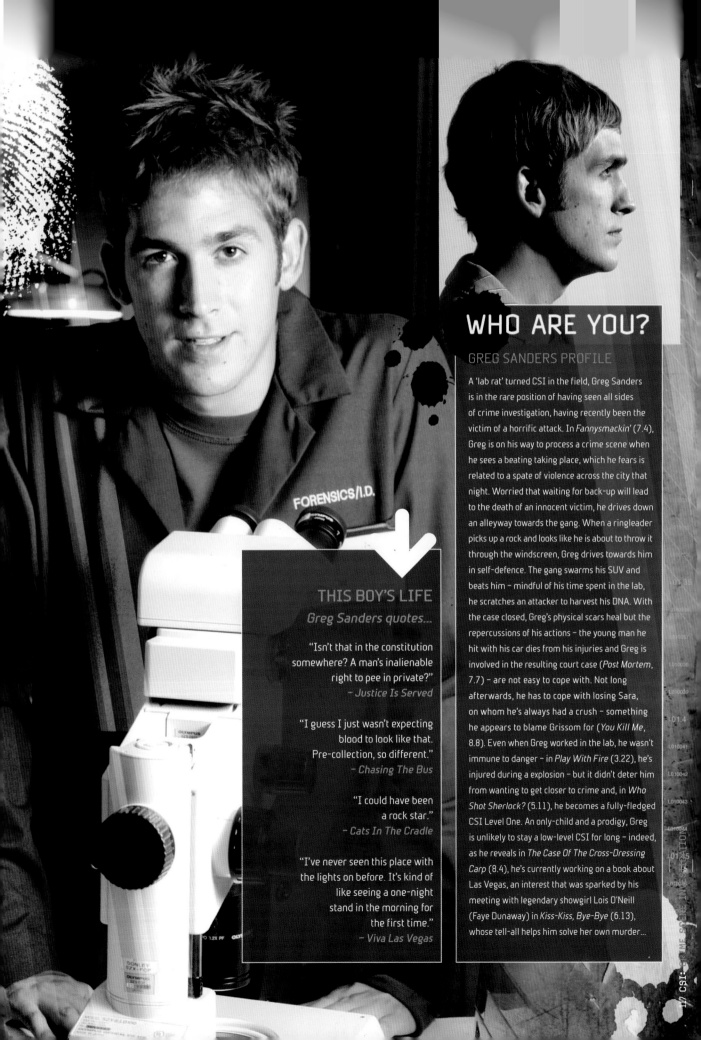

WHO ARE YOU?

GREG SANDERS PROFILE

A 'lab rat' turned CSI in the field, Greg Sanders is in the rare position of having seen all sides of crime investigation, having recently been the victim of a horrific attack. In *Fannysmackin'* (7.4), Greg is on his way to process a crime scene when he sees a beating taking place, which he fears is related to a spate of violence across the city that night. Worried that waiting for back-up will lead to the death of an innocent victim, he drives down an alleyway towards the gang. When a ringleader picks up a rock and looks like he is about to throw it through the windscreen, Greg drives towards him in self-defence. The gang swarms his SUV and beats him – mindful of his time spent in the lab, he scratches an attacker to harvest his DNA. With the case closed, Greg's physical scars heal but the repercussions of his actions – the young man he hit with his car dies from his injuries and Greg is involved in the resulting court case (*Post Mortem*, 7.7) – are not easy to cope with. Not long afterwards, he has to cope with losing Sara, on whom he's always had a crush – something he appears to blame Grissom for (*You Kill Me*, 8.8). Even when Greg worked in the lab, he wasn't immune to danger – in *Play With Fire* (3.22), he's injured during a explosion – but it didn't deter him from wanting to get closer to crime and, in *Who Shot Sherlock?* (5.11), he becomes a fully-fledged CSI Level One. An only-child and a prodigy, Greg is unlikely to stay a low-level CSI for long – indeed, as he reveals in *The Case Of The Cross-Dressing Carp* (8.4), he's currently working on a book about Las Vegas, an interest that was sparked by his meeting with legendary showgirl Lois O'Neill (Faye Dunaway) in *Kiss-Kiss, Bye-Bye* (6.13), whose tell-all helps him solve her own murder...

THIS BOY'S LIFE
Greg Sanders quotes....

"Isn't that in the constitution somewhere? A man's inalienable right to pee in private?"
– *Justice Is Served*

"I guess I just wasn't expecting blood to look like that. Pre-collection, so different."
– *Chasing The Bus*

"I could have been a rock star."
– *Cats In The Cradle*

"I've never seen this place with the lights on before. It's kind of like seeing a one-night stand in the morning for the first time."
– *Viva Las Vegas*

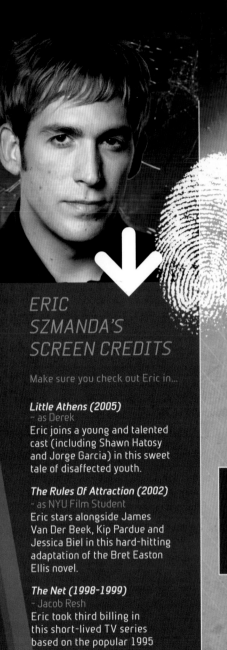

are doing a rape kit together. Although it wasn't in the script at all, I saw an opportunity to flirt with her in what most people would consider a non-sexual situation. Because we do this kind of stuff everyday in *CSI* world, we don't have the same taboos. And Marg Helgenberger totally responded to it. I remember the director wasn't into it at all and didn't know where it was coming from. I think maybe he was new at the time and didn't understand the character relationships. He agreed it added some color to the scene and he allowed us to keep it so it became an ongoing thing. The same goes for Greg and Sara or Greg and any female on the show. He's tried at least once with all of them even though his ongoing infatuation with Catherine is still there.

On top of that, Greg's trademark was his haircuts and sense of style. Where did those originate from?
I guess that was my idea. When I auditioned, I was asked to be myself. Greg's sense of style isn't that far off from mine. A lot of it was inspired by the fact that I was covered by a lab coat and I wanted to do something that would make me stand out. Greg's an individual who thinks outside the box so he would like to shock people with a hairstyle or a creepy outfit just to get a reaction out of them. It worked to my

It is easy to look at his antics, but was Greg always striving to prove himself to the others?
In terms of Greg's background, he's always been ahead of his class, but also the youngest in his field. Obviously, his appearance probably gives people the wrong impression, that he's not diligent or efficient. So yeah, he's always seeking the approval of Grissom, as most of the CSIs are, and Greg is the rookie so he does have a lot to prove. And he wants to do well at his job so I don't think that part will ever go away.

It was your suggestion that Greg graduate to full time CSI. Was it a difficult sell to the producers?
Looking back, I still wonder what got into me. I went into that meeting and suggested that but because it came from such an organic place, you really would believe Greg was going stir crazy in the lab and was curious to see what it was like on the outside. In the real world, CSIs wouldn't go from a lab position to a field position; it would be the other way around and there would be a pay increase. So they were kind of playing against reality but I saw a great opportunity for the writers to take the viewers on the adventures of being a rookie. I got to be the eyes for the audience and learn with them. I am obviously glad they took me up on it but I do think it was

> **"If it weren't for Sara's relationship with Grissom, I would hope Greg would have been runner up.**

advantage as an actor because it made me stand out in the cast. I've enjoyed continuing that same idea but I also have to think more in terms of what it is like to be in the field. Appearance plays a part of that so I've tried to tone it down over the last couple of seasons.

Speaking of standing out, one of Greg's most notorious moments was when he was caught dancing with the headdress on. How did you approach that scene?
That was on the page and I believe Danny Cannon was the director of that episode. He was also the director of the pilot that helped me create the character and gave me the freedom to do whatever came to me. I remember that being on the page and thinking, "I can't believe they want me to do this, but I will do it." After we did it, one of the background actors came up to me and said, "You do realize 50 million people are going to see what you just did." It hit me like, "Wow! These little moments of insanity are going to be remembered forever!" I enjoy doing stuff like that and bringing that kind of levity to the show when everything is really serious. I hope I get to continue doing that.

driven by something that came from the character as opposed to an actor just wanting more screen time.

Grissom has been both hard and nurturing when it comes to Greg. What's your take on their relationship?
Well, Grissom sees a little bit of himself in Greg. I don't want to speak for him but that is why Greg takes it a little bit farther than most people would with Grissom. And I think Grissom gives him a little bit of freedom because he does see his potential to excel in the field. Both of us tend to think outside of the box which helps define some common ground. A lot of those relationships you see on screen came from something you couldn't necessarily write and it is just that special thing that happens between actors.

Greg teamed up with Sara quite a bit in the fifth season. Did you feel a spark develop between them?
Yeah, of course. Greg was very open about his desire to get to know Sara. Greg looked forward to every opportunity to work on a case with her and be under her wing. For a while, I was rooting for that as well but we all know how that worked out.

Considering his flirtations with both of them, who would be better suited for Greg – Catherine or Sara? I think Catherine could teach Greg a few things and conversely, Greg could teach Catherine a thing or two. And if it weren't for Sara's relationship with Grissom, I would hope Greg would have been runner up. There is something special between them but that might have turned into a brotherly thing.

Last season, a big episode for Greg was *Fannysmackin'*. What was your reaction to that script?
Well, luckily the producers called me ahead of time and told me what the story arc would entail so that when I read the script, I wouldn't have a heart attack. But I was really excited about doing something different and getting dirty on the job. I liked the characteristics that were displayed by Greg. I got to work with one of my favorite directors, Richard Lewis. I always trust he's going to make the best of it. And I am happy with the way it turned out. I got to do some of my own stunts, get thrown to the ground, get kicked, and then left for dead. Then the scene in the hospital afterwards revealed some vulnerability in my character which is very important.

Did you agree with Greg's drastic measures?
Greg did the best with what he had at that moment and what he had to do. Obviously, that was questioned by the authorities but Greg's motivation for plowing down that kid was to save someone else's life which is part of the job description. Greg doesn't get to carry a weapon and didn't have any other way of making the assailant stop. Personally, I would have liked to have done something else than run a small kid over with a huge truck but you never know what you are going to do in a situation where you only have a second to respond. Looking back, I don't know if there were any other options. Unfortunately, it didn't work out exactly as he planned but it wasn't intentional.

CSI has spawned trading cards, a comic book, and video and board games, so what should a Greg Sanders action figure look like and do?
It should be able to dance, have a good hairstyle, a nice wardrobe, and do math for you. CSI

TRIVIA

Although Eric is of Polish descent, he actually grew up in the state of Wisconsin.

MODEL MURDERER

In season seven, Grissom met his match in the petite form of Natalie Davis a.k.a. The Miniature Killer. JESSICA COLLINS, the actress behind this ingenious and deeply troubled murderess, speaks exclusively about her time on the show.

Natalie Davis – a killer with attention to detail matched only by Grissom himself; the serial psycho who left dainty dollhouse crime-scene replicas in her murderous wake – certainly gave the Vegas CSIs a run for their money in season seven. When they finally caught her, a few body bags later, they were as shocked as us to discover the cold-blooded killer was a plain-looking girl with an unhealthy attachment to bleach. Perhaps their confusion had something to do with the fact that, at first, the folks at *CSI* Central weren't sure who they wanted the killer to be either…

"I think the creative team were trying to find out who The Miniature Killer was themselves," explains Jessica Collins, the actress whose creepy rendition of "I've Got A Pain In My Sawdust" will haunt *CSI* viewers for many years to come. "They came to the conclusion they wanted her to be a woman, so when I auditioned, and they liked what I was offering, there was a lot of freedom to create the character. I met with the writers and we talked about Natalie and who she was. It was a very collaborative effort – something I've never experienced on a show before."

The 26-year-old Texan actress knew that the character of Natalie would be a big pay-off for the audience who had followed her crimes throughout the season, and took that responsibility very seriously. "I worked hard to prepare for the role," Collins says. "I looked at real-life female serial killers, and researched schizophrenia. I also used

my imagination, as I wanted to create something unique and different. For a character like that, there's not exactly a breakdown to follow."

Having worked hard with the writers to develop a dramatic and destructive background for Natalie, Collins wasn't fazed when she showed up to shoot her scenes. "It made me feel very comfortable that I didn't have to try and be something I had no idea about. Natalie could be what I had to offer."

Surely William Petersen's presence had her feeling a little nervy, especially in their one-on-one scenes? "Those scenes were very intense, but Bill is such a fantastic actor. He's just so smart, and funny, and the crew loves him. I think he's one of the reasons the show is adored, because he truly works hard to produce an amazing product."

So it's no surprise when Collins tells us her favorite scene was where Grissom confronts Natalie to find out where she's hidden Sara. "In a way, Natalie is Grissom's equal in genius. It's almost as if they function on different ends of the spectrum. They're very well matched and it's interesting to play those opposites. That scene was fun because I got to sort of listen and be affected by what he had to say. Bill did most of the work. I did the slicing of his throat and the singing, but he really did the bulk of the acting work in that one!"

Collins' modesty doesn't slip by unnoticed. And we make sure she knows just how creepy we found her singing! "It was creepy!" she laughs.

"I remember getting an old version of the song that sounded like it was on a record player. I had to listen to it in my apartment over and over to try and learn it. One of my friends thinks it's the scariest thing ever. She can't watch it or listen to it or she says she won't be able to hang out with me anymore!"

Refusing to acknowledge her own impressive input into The Miniature Killer arc, Collins is quick to praise the production department for their creative work on Natalie's lair. "It was so beautiful and intricate. That set absolutely helped me get into Natalie's mind. Looking at a bunch of severed dolls' heads in a jar will pretty much do the trick! I loved that when she was alone in that apartment she's working in this world with dolls everywhere, and, to her, it's a perfect little universe, but when it's raided by the CSI team, it's not; it's dingy and dark and scary."

Despite playing one of the most messed up murderers on the show, Collins' time on *CSI* was far from miserable, even if the crew didn't always know what to make of her. "I don't know if they knew how to approach me," she admits, "because it had been built up, and then I arrived on set and everybody would be looking at me, saying, 'That's the Miniature Killer!' Crewmembers would come up to me and whisper, 'I think we need to wire you. Is that okay?' I think it really cracked the producers up after each take, because I'd go from this weird, creepy character, and then look over and smile at them

"CSI was a fantastic, enriching, challenging, and eye-opening experience." >>>

and just snap back into who I really am. I think everyone was like, 'She's actually nice!'"

Those crewmembers probably felt more comfortable when Collins returned in season nine to film Natalie's court hearing, an ending for her character the actress feels was fitting. "I think it's a great end. It really bookends her killing spree. I read somewhere that by hanging herself, the [first letters of the methods used] in each of her killings spell out the word BLEACH. It was nice to be in Grissom's final season as well."

Nowadays, Collins has left the dingy world of serial killing behind and has taken on the role of

a "sweet girl" in a political thriller pilot series for AMC called *Rubicon*. "It's an action show, so it was cool to film, and we shot it in New York on location. I think it's going to be really awesome," Collins assures us with such enthusiasm we're certain it will be. But she still remembers her time on *CSI* fondly. "Even though I was playing this horrific murderess, it was a pleasant experience," she laughs. "Everyone is such a team over there. It was a fantastic, enriching, challenging, and eye-opening experience. *CSI* is the number one show on television," Collins concludes, matter-of-factly, "who wouldn't want to do it?" CSI

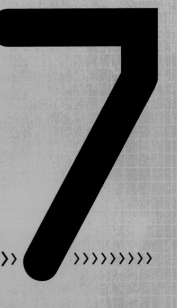

SEASON

CSI
SCRAP BOOK

Happy memories: (above) the *Vegas* cast and crew gather to say goodbye to William Petersen; (right) Jorja Fox makes a wordless cameo in Petersen's final episode, *One To Go*; (below) David Berman and Robert David Hall share a joke.

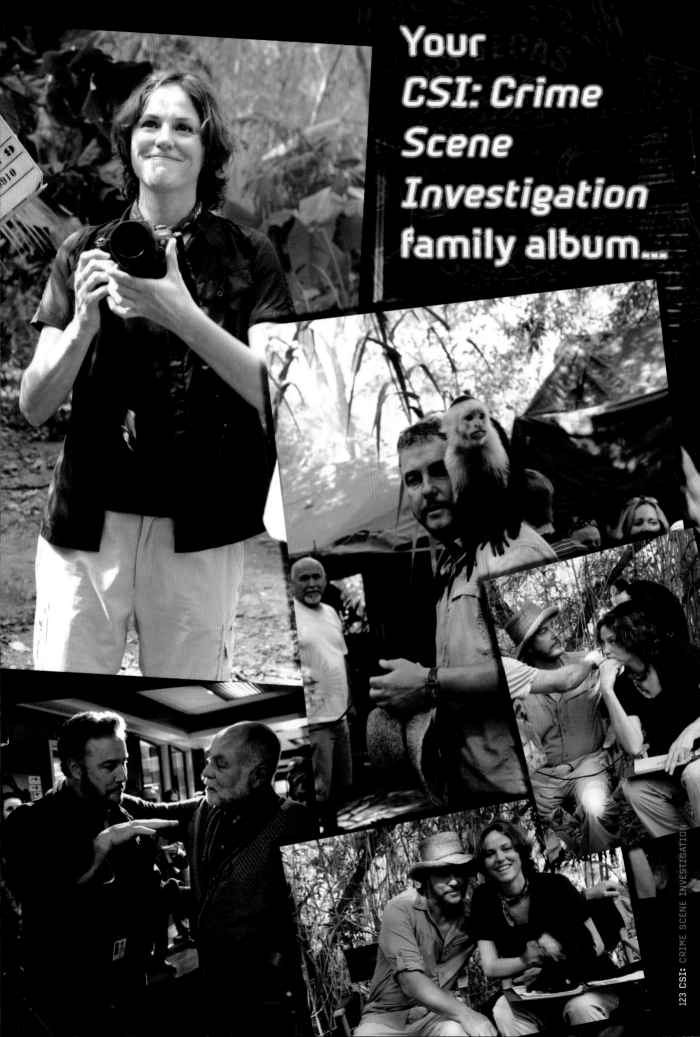

Your
CSI: Crime
Scene
Investigation
family album...

Monkeying around: (left) William Petersen films his final scenes; (below right) Marg Helgenberger prepares for a take; (below) Billy makes a new friend.

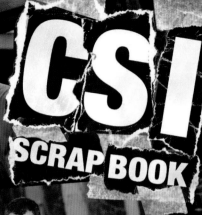

CSI
SCRAP BOOK

CSI SCRAP BOOK

Final check:
(above) Paul
Guilfoyle and Marg
Helgenberger run
through their lines;
(left) George Eads
shares a joke with Marg
and Lauren Lee Smith.

Lady in red: (below) Laurence Fishburne surveys a particularly gruesome crime scene in the 200th episode *Mascara*, directed by William Friedkin (below left).

STROKE OF GENIUS

Love him or hate him, David Hodges is impossible to ignore, be it his accidental putdowns (remember when he described fellow lab tech Wendy Simms as "clumsy but buxom") or his sycophantic tendencies towards boss Gil Grissom. Here, actor Wallace Langham, who became a cast regular in season eight of *CSI: Crime Scene Investigation*, reveals what makes the irrepressible Hodges tick...

If we can take you right the way back to your first few episodes of *CSI: Crime Scene Investigation*, how did you get the enviable role of David Hodges?
There was originally a trace tech played by an actor named Eddie Jemison who's in the *Ocean's Eleven* movies, and a terrific actor. When they called to bring him back he wasn't available because he was shooting a film. We happen to share the same manager, and our manager suggested me, and they thought it was a good idea. They changed the name and brought me in. I got to work with William Petersen, and I guess they liked me enough to bring me back a little while later, and it snowballed from there.

What did you like about the character?

I liked the fact that he was really trying to connect with the boss, sometimes in a very misguided way, and that the work seemed secondary to him.

Was Hodges written the way he's portrayed on screen, or did you bring his eccentricities to the role yourself?
It's a little bit of both. I think that once the writers saw my take on it and what I could do, we got to play around with whether Hodges has major problems with socialization or whether he really makes an attempt at it, or whether, you know, he couldn't care less. On any given day, at any given moment, it could be one or a combination of all of those things.

Tell us about the little dance from season seven. That was a lovely touch...
That was the director Richard Lewis, who is never afraid to make a suggestion, just to keep things fresh. He said, "Why don't you dance?" And I said, "What, just go ahead and dance?" And he said, "Yeah, just do something." So I just started making something up and nobody told me to stop, so I kept going. We did it a few times actually and I got more and more embarrassed by the moment, but what they come up with is fantastic.

What, in your opinion, is Hodges' function on the show?
I think, technically, he's obviously there for trace evidence. But, in the context of the show, I think that Hodges really brings a texture that is not so serious to some very serious plotlines and stories. I personally think that it's important to break up the drama with something that has some humor or some kind of comedy to it, because if it's all drama, all of the time, I think it would get too heavy for people.

Would you like to see Hodges in the field more?
I'm really just happy where they put me to be honest. Yeah, it would be fun to get outdoors sometimes, but I'm also very content just in my contained little world in the lab. Our set is pretty amazing to walk into and be a part of. It almost feels like a home when you walk in – you know where things are. You can reach into a drawer and grab something and you know where this goes and that goes. There's a familiarity to it that I think is comfortable for me. But I love that they put Hodges out in the field to take him out of his element and that's fun to play because he's a fish out of water at that point and it is like a whole new world for him. He likes to pretend that he knows what he's doing, but he really has no idea.

How are you with the technical jargon?
It was a struggle at the beginning because I don't have a science background, but we have amazing technical advisors and they're very smart when they write – they break the Latin down phonetically. So I can actually learn to pronounce what I'm saying. I really enjoy finding out what I'm talking about actually – I don't mind doing some research into certain conifers, or what type of chemical component makes up a truck tire, or whatever. The science is extremely important to our producers. Even though we're doing a truncated Hollywood version of the process, we try to adhere to what would actually go on in a trace lab, or how they actually would process things, and how the science does help them to solve crimes.

Do you recall the things you're learning? Or is it in one ear, out the other, so to speak?
Well, the funny thing is, if I learn something and it comes up in conversation, I can speak with some small amount of knowledge about it. And I certainly didn't have that ability before. It's been great to be able to learn more...

That knowledge must come in handy at dinner parties...
It can, although I have to admit I do tend to forget some of it because I have to move on to the next storyline. So I put it out of my head and put something else in there...

As you've mentioned, Hodges, in many ways, is the show's comic relief. Do you struggle to keep a straight face during some of his scenes?
Absolutely. We try to have as much fun as possible and I find that when I work with George

TRIVIA
Wallace met his first wife Laura on the set of the 1985 movie *Weird Science*. Just over 18 months later they were married.

Wallace can be seen and heard as Dr. Grant Seeker in the Dinosaur ride at Disney's Animal Kingdom in Orlando, Florida.

Eads especially, that we definitely try to make each other laugh. None of it ever gets on screen, because it's very serious, it's about solving crime, but, yeah, we're having a really good time.

What would you like to see happen to Hodges over the next few seasons?
I would love to find out more about Hodges personally. You know, get him a girlfriend, or spark a relationship at the lab. To have something that he has to struggle with on a personal basis. I think Hodges' main defect is that he feels that he's very adept socially, when he's actually very inept. So I think adding the romantic element to it would actually kind of turn his world upside down a little bit.

Is there anyone in particular you'd like to see Hodges get together with?
We've been exploring things with Wendy a little bit. I don't know how far they want to take it though.

Are you surprised at how popular Hodges has proved with *CSI* fans?
It's interesting, I was talking to a friend of mine about this the other day and as an actor I find that I work in a vacuum. I go to work, I shoot my scenes, I go home. Then a few weeks later I get to watch it on television. I don't realize that there are millions of other people also doing the same thing, so it's still kind of surprising that people know who I am. I'm really happy about it and really pleased to be a part of something so popular.

Do people approach you in the street?
They do. I get a lot of people who think they've met me before. It's less of, "Oh, you're Hodges from *CSI*," and more, "We've met before," and I have to tell them: "No, I don't think we have!"

Did you find it daunting joining a show that was already such a success?
I think the thing that was daunting for me was

WHO ARE YOU?

DAVID HODGES PROFILE

LAPD import David Hodges can't be faulted on his technical ability but his social skills leave much to be desired. He believes his trace analysis to be of far greater importance to the lab than other fields; when a crew shoots inside the lab in *I Like To Watch* (6.17), he scoffs, "That's a waste of film" as they point their lens at Archie Johnson in the A/V lab, then pages the cameramen so they arrive in time to capture him delivering findings to Sara Sidle. Hodges' greatest ambition is to be considered a peer by Grissom, who he openly idolizes; when Gil leaves his office unattended in *Lab Rats* (7.20), Hodges corals his fellow technicians and they re-examine the Miniature Killer's models, trying to identify details the CSIs might have missed. When Hodges tells Grissom he found a bleach link between all four models, Grissom is impressed: "Good job, Hodges. Really."

Hodges reunites the tech staff once again for *You Kill Me* (8.8), in which he tests their detective skills with a series of unlikely crime-scene scenarios that turn out to be the basis for a board game he's developing called Lab Rats. Grissom, perhaps glad of a distraction from missing or being asked about Sara, is glad to play along with Hodges – but in this instance, it was DNA technician Wendy Simms he was really trying to impress, even if he went about it the wrong way, making a spoof figurine of her describing her as "clumsy but buxom". Perhaps his lack of success with a real-life lady is to be expected – when, aged 17, he tried to pick up a prostitute, it turned out to be an undercover policewoman and he had to get his mother to pick him up from the station...

just understanding what the show was about and how the tone went, and the rhythms and the technical jargon. To be honest, I'd never seen the show before I did it. I knew it was popular, I knew it was a success, but it was just the type of television that I wasn't watching at the time. That's not to say it was good or bad, it's a very good show, I just didn't have time to catch an episode, because I got the job and went to work the next day, so I was coming in very fresh. But the popularity of it is something that exists outside of the atmosphere of the set and our studio. When you go onto the set, everybody is very nice and very warm and there's no ego involved. It's really kind of refreshing to go to work and know that you're on one of the most popular shows in television history, but nobody's acting as if that's a factor.

Would you say the cast and crew chemistry is the reason for the show's popularity?
I think it's the sole reason. Well, I can't say it's the sole reason, I think that the people who watch the show make it a success, but what makes it a comfortable and pleasant environment to work in is the fact that William

What did you think about all the fan speculation that Hodges was the Miniature Killer? Did it cross your mind that he might be?
Well, I thought it was a great red herring. It was something that the writers kept telling me that they consciously wanted to subconsciously plant in the fans' minds. Hodges is just twisted enough that this may actually be a factor. I always thought the thing about Hodges at his core is that we're glad he's working in law enforcement, because he's just weird enough to really be a problem. But I'm very glad I wasn't the Miniature Killer because I'd be out of a job.

We have to ask... what do you think Hodges does when he goes home from work at the end of the day?
I would imagine he spends a good amount of time obsessing about how he may have upset someone during the day. Or not. I think he replays conversations in his head for a little while and then realizes, okay, my day was fine, I can let it go. And then I think he's playing video games or making dinner. I don't see a lot of social life for Hodges. But I think he does have quirky hobbies for sure.

"I'm very glad I wasn't the Miniature Killer because I'd be out of a job."

Petersen and Marg Helgenberger and our showrunners Carol Mendelsohn and Naren Shankar are all just fantastically pleasant, personable people.

***Lab Rats* is easily Hodges' standout episode to date. What are your memories of this particular instalment?**
That was a lot of fun. I think this was a pet project of the writers for many years. They'd been wanting to do this for a few seasons, and I think it finally came together last season because they'd gotten the right ensemble of lab techs, you know, people who've stood the test of time. It's tough to do that job as an actor, and if you look at the course of the show, there are so many people who've come on, and then moved on... I think this was the first time the writers were able to look at the collection of talent they had and really think, "Yeah, this could work as an episode!"

Do you think he'll ever fulfil his dream of stepping into Grissom's shoes?
If the time was right for Hodges to step up to the plate and fill those shoes, I think he'd be ready for it. He'd be ready for it until something came his way and knocked him off kilter. I think there may be a sense of pretending (that he could do the job all on his own) and then the realization that he actually can't, and that he has a very good team of CSIs. I think that initial over-compensation may be a problem.

Finally, stepping away from *CSI*, what else are you working on at the moment?
The last thing that I did was *The Great Buck Howard*, which was a film with John Malkovich (see box out). And I also recently directed a play in Los Angeles, which was a lot more work than I imagined, so I'm a little exhausted. I have two teenagers and a young daughter, and a wife who I never see. CSI

THE GREAT BUCK HOWARD

Wallace Langham tells us about his latest big screen endeavour...

"The last thing that I did was *The Great Buck Howard*, which was a film with John Malkovich, Colin Hanks and a man named Ricky Jay. John Malkovich plays a washed up mentalist who was very popular in the 1960s, '70s and '80s and made frequent appearances on American television shows such as *The Merv Griffin Show* and *Johnny Carson*. He's someone who can read minds and do magic and things like that, but he's down on his luck by this point and trying to make a comeback. Then this young kid comes to Los Angeles and falls into being his tour manager and you get to watch the character of Buck getting closer and closer to his shot – that shot being that he gets a tryout at a casino in Vegas. I play one of the producers of the casino show in Vegas. It seems like I can't work anywhere but there..."

LIFE ACCORDING TO HODGES

The man really does have a way with words!

"Every man is not an end, but a beginning. Today I rise above and step up. Have a nice day."
– *Lab Rats*

"Look I'm sure Grissom's told you, well maybe not you, but he's told me many times that we speak for the dead. Think of this exercise as a way for the dead to speak for themselves."
– *You Kill Me*

"Do I look like the Ghost Whisperer?"
– *The Case Of The Cross Dressing Carp*

LAB RATS

010036
L010037
L010038
L010039
L01.4
L010041
L010042

"It really feels that episodes such as Lab Rats are our special time. When the cat's away the mice will play!"
– Archie Kao

← "Quotation"

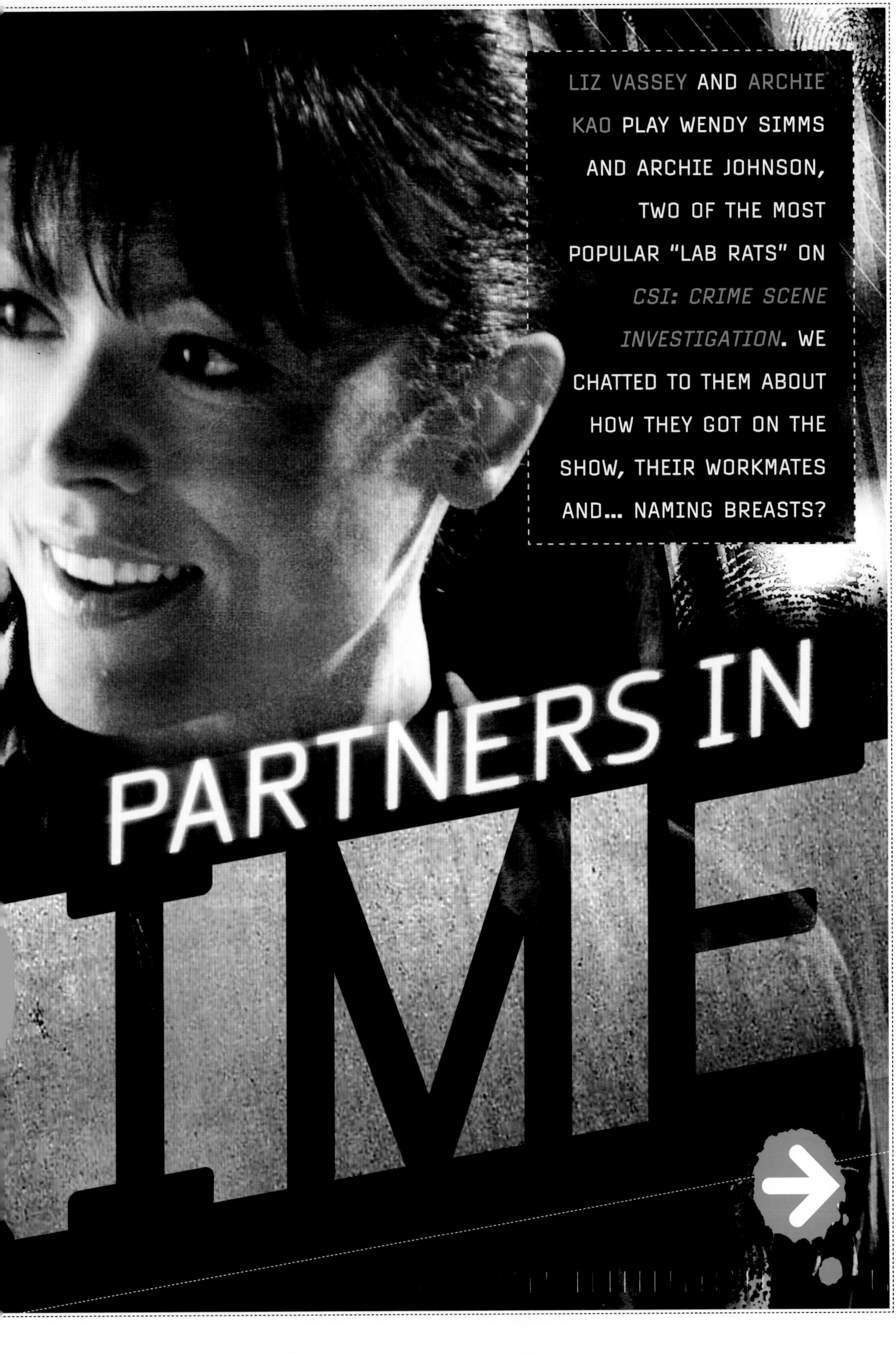

PARTNERS IN IME

LIZ VASSEY AND ARCHIE KAO PLAY WENDY SIMMS AND ARCHIE JOHNSON, TWO OF THE MOST POPULAR "LAB RATS" ON *CSI: CRIME SCENE INVESTIGATION*. WE CHATTED TO THEM ABOUT HOW THEY GOT ON THE SHOW, THEIR WORKMATES AND... NAMING BREASTS?

↓ "Quotation"

> ## "I keep begging to do a musical episode. If it happens, I'll do a rousing ballad called 'Seven Epithelials In Common.'" – Liz Vassey

They may not exactly get the same screen time as, say, Gil Grissom or Catherine Willows, but *CSI: Crime Scene Investigation*'s lab team is the heart and soul of the operation. The likes of Wallace Langham (David Hodges), John Wellner (Henry Andrews), Liz Vassey, and Archie Kao have become so popular that the producers have started basing entire episodes – such as *Lab Rats* and last season's *You Kill Me* – around the antics of the tireless test tube experts. And considering that the people who play them are all funny, down-to-earth types who appreciate the lucky break the show has been for their careers, it's not exactly a tough job to interview them. The hard part is trying not to choke from laughing. So getting to talk with Liz Vassey (who plays "nerdy guy in a woman's body" Wendy Simms) and Archie Kao (audio-visual tech guru Archie Johnson) is naturally a fun time. The pair came to *CSI: Crime Scene Investigation* after ploughing away on other TV shows, with Vassey notching up an impressive résumé of guest appearances and Kao making his way modeling and taking small roles. Both admit that the lab is an easy place to work, given the company.

"I think co-dependency describes the relationship between the lab guys!" laughs Vassey. "I think David Berman (coroner's assistant David Phillips) and I talk about 14 times a day. We decided we would be best friends and now we kind of are. Wally (Langham) and I would happily work together with nobody else for the rest of our lives. I couldn't respect him more, but I wouldn't want you to tell him that."

They especially seem to appreciate the chance to run a little wild with the lab-set shows. "It really feels that episodes such as *Lab Rats* are our special time," says Kao. "We really enjoy each other's company and when the cat's away the mice will play! We have the run of the studio and it's always funny. They really encourage that. And Naren Shankar said he thinks there should be one every season. I'm hoping that will be the case. He's mentioned in seasons past about how he would like to see the lab be a living, breathing place, where the characters are not simply vehicles for exposition. When I read *You Kill Me*, I marveled at the genius of the writing."

Liz Vassey got her start at the tender age of nine, winning the leading role of Oliver Twist in a local musical, despite her mother's fears that the shy little girl would be better off in the chorus. She blossomed on stage, however, quickly finding her feet, and ended up appearing in several theater productions before she realized she needed to focus on her academic life... "At 15, I got a manager in New York and started flying back and forth for auditions. I got a national tour of *Evita*, which I then couldn't do because I thought graduating from high school might be a good idea," she says, before relating the story of how she essentially fell into the world of TV. "I auditioned for the daytime soap *All My Children* for a lark and they called me back many times. And then they said they needed a singer for the role so I had to go in and sing. I had to do a seduction scene at age 16 and I'm a minister's daughter from Florida so I didn't even get that it was seductive. I'm approaching this guy with an ice cube saying, 'It's so hot in here, can you rub this on my back...?' And I was thinking, 'Well, it might be hot in there, that might be a smart idea...'"

For Kao, the route was a little different – a mix of adverts, guest shots, and modeling, before landing a lead role in a hugely popular, but hardly Shakespearian production... "*Power Rangers*," he laughs. "I was Blue Ranger. It's funny, I was at a mall recently and this little boy and his mom recognized me. He knew me from *Power Rangers* and she knew

LIZ TRIVIA Liz loves animals, and shares her home with two rescued dogs and two rescued cats. She's also a huge science-fiction fan.

me from *CSI*, and they both wanted autographs for the different shows. I signed autographs as two different characters at the same time!" While acting in spandex might not sound like the best way to improve your serious acting career, Kao credits it with helping him learn the tools of the trade on camera. "It was a great way to get experience in front of the camera. If you show up and work in front of the camera every day, you're going to get better at it."

Vassey, meanwhile, moved on from soap land, traveled cross-country to LA and landed numerous small roles, including two appearances each on *Quantum Leap* and *Murder She Wrote*. Despite a run of bad luck with several shows getting canceled after a few episodes, she's grateful for the experience.

"I know how lucky I am – I have so many friends who should be working but aren't and I can't be frustrated about the shows that were canceled swiftly. I look at it like this: I've been a working actor for 20 years now and I find a lot of happiness in that. The ones that stopped early were quirky and odd and weird and I loved them. I just wish networks had a little more patience.

which one she wanted me to fix by their names. So it comes out in *Stuff* magazine and I had every ex-boyfriend calling me up saying, 'You couldn't have picked my name?' I didn't really name them!"

The endless audition process she's endured over the years almost made Vassey skip the chance to appear on *CSI* altogether. "Wendy was kind of weird. It was 2005 and I had gone to a lot of auditions and gotten to the network reading stage 15 times, which was great on the one hand because I was getting that close, but I'd always lose out on the part. I was so fed up with working my ass off to get a job and not getting it. This thing came up to audition for *CSI* and originally they wanted a person of a certain ethnicity for that role – someone who was Asian. But they were open to other people. I'd heard that before so I didn't want to go in for it. Finally, after they asked me a few times, I had my husband – who is this incredible camera operator who works with James Cameron – shoot an audition tape for me. Short of a wind machine, I couldn't find anyone to make me look better. We shot it in the front

ARCHIE TRIVIA Archie graduated from George Mason University with a degree in speech communication.

I actually auditioned for another role on the show and didn't get it. It was for the handwriting analysis expert. At the time, I was doing a movie and didn't think much about the show – I had never heard of it. It was just another audition. I heard that my agent had had talks and that the *CSI* guys liked me and they were going to find something for me. I thought, 'Right...' You hear that all the time. But true to form, Carol found something for me and it grew from there. It really worked out! I work far more than the hand writing analysis guy! In fact, last season they showed Archie going into that lab and taking over that role!"

And so to their work on the show. Vassey, alongside David Berman, will become a regular on the show in the ninth season and it'll give her some extra plotlines. But she admits she loves the science stuff she usually deals with. "I'm interested in the science stuff. I've read books on it and find it fascinating. I always want to know what I'm doing."

Kao's also comfortable with his job: "In all honesty, I feel pretty happy with the tech stuff. What can be a challenge is shooting out of order. We don't always have the visual component for what we're referring to. So sometimes we're staring at a green screen, or I'm just staring at a tape mark on a blank monitor and we're just imagining what's going on. So that becomes a technical challenge."

He also admits that he's not the best with a keyboard. "I'm not a good typist. There's this guy, Mark Weinman, who works the audio-visual equipment for when I'm doing a scene. I call him the guy behind the guy. He bridges the gap!"

Finally, if you'll indulge us, we'd like to launch a campaign on behalf of Liz Vassey. The musical-obsessed actress, who crops up as a member of the Evil League Of Evil in Joss Whedon's *Dr. Horrible*, has been hoping for a song-and-dance *CSI* episode for years now. "I'm a huge fan of the *Buffy* musical and I've been trying to talk to them about it – if they could do it with vampires I'm sure they could do it with scientists. I keep begging but I don't know if it'll ever happen! If it does, I'll do a rousing ballad called 'Seven Epithelials In Common.' It'll bring down the whole second act. I worry it would send most people, apart from Robert David Hall and myself, away in panic, but I think Billy Petersen should do interpretive dance."

The push for 'Once More With Epithelials' starts here, folks... CSI

I think *The Tick* was actually, even if I didn't have a lot to do with it, an incredible show."

The live-action version of Ben Edlund's goofy comic book, *The Tick*, was one of those that succumbed to network impatience, but remains a particular favorite in its many fans' minds – and Vassey's. Appearing as the corset-wearing heroine Captain Liberty remains one of her favorite TV experiences, even if she did manage to start a certain urban legend – namely that she named her breasts during costume changes. "Okay, I'm going to set the breasts thing straight! Whenever anything had to be fixed in the Captain Liberty costume, the costume lady would talk about

room, and a cat walks by at one point and there's a pool guy outside... I sent in the tape and thought that would stop them asking. They asked again! They wanted 'the girl from the house.' I hadn't seen the show and didn't know who (executive producer) Carol Mendelsohn was when I read. They told me within two hours that the job was mine. It was the best breath of fresh air."

Kao doesn't have any breast-naming stories (at least, we don't think he does), but he does have his own audition tale. "I didn't actually audition for the role of Archie Johnson. They created the role for me, I think. I don't really know where the name comes from. I'm going to have to ask Carol Mendelsohn.

SEASON EIGHT: ↘
INTERVIEW

TRIGGER HAPPY

If you want to see some of Gerald's *CSI* inspired comedy, check out his myspace: www.myspace.com/itsahardg or say hi at www.gerald.biz.

In season eight's *You Kill Me*, Bobby Dawson, the gun guy, felt the wrath of Hodges, fictional as it was. Actor and comedian GERALD (with a hard G) MCCULLOUCH talks oddballs, stand-up, and what he'd really like to do with the LVPD's most annoying lab rat.

How did you get involved with *CSI*? I got involved by just going to an audition for the very first episode, after the pilot. I had no idea what that audition would mean down the road or the importance it would have in my life. It totally changed my life! No one had any idea that it would become this iconic television show.

Having been a recurring character for so long, was it exciting to have a script based around the lab-techs? I loved the script – it was totally different from the other scripts, and it was kind of fun to be the focal point. I didn't get to have the experience of working with the other lab techs because they were all together on days when I wasn't there – I didn't get any time to really sit and talk to them about what they thought. My reality – Bobby's story – is isolated from everyone else's; all my stuff was shot on one day. It was a very quick day, and most of my scenes are with Brass. Because I was in a different reality to everyone else, I guess I had to exist under different circumstances.

When the script for *You Kill Me* came in, did you notice that Hodges really doesn't like Bobby much? Bobby does get picked on a lot! I don't get it, there are the other lab techs, and then there's

Bobby way off to the left! So I read it and I thought, "It figures I'm the oddball!" I guess Bobby *is* kind of the misfit of the lab techs. I want Bobby to retort to Hodges – that's what I want! There have been a few times that Hodges has thrown some jabs at Bobby, and I'm never given anything to say back to him, so Bobby just has to take it! Why does Bobby have to be so submissive? I guess Hodges just has it in for me. Maybe one day we'll duke it out... I'm sure Bobby would win hands down! Throw Hodges an uppercut or something like that – knock him out and just go about my business. The one thing I was most excited about was that Paris Barclay directed the episode. He's a prolific director who I have a lot of respect for, and who I'd wanted to work with for many years. I was so excited when I got the script and saw that he was directing it. I was really honored and thankful to have had that experience.

Did you have much leeway with the script? I didn't really. I live in New York and LA – I go back and forth, so my travel schedule is hectic and sometimes I don't get the script until I land in LA only hours prior to shooting.

Because I got the script so close to when we shot, I didn't really have the luxury of time to investigate where else I could have gone, other than what was in the script – it was definitely a time for me to really stay focused and stay present! I just had to go for it and let the story dictate where I went. I think I may have come across as a wimp! Maybe as an actor I should have stayed up all night and investigated how else Bobby could react, which I've had to do before for some episodes! I think everyone liked it and had a lot of fun watching it, though.

What's it like being part of the biggest television show in the world? It's a trip! It's something that I just didn't expect when it started nine years ago and it has impacted my life in a way that no other job ever has. I also do stand-up comedy, using my nine years of experience as the "misfit gun guy," and there's definitely a common knowledge that the audience and I share about *CSI*. It's kind of fun to spin that from my perspective, and I think the audience gets a kick out of it! The show changed my life and the impact it's had is indescribable. It's become such a part of my day-to-day existence and it's affected all aspects of my life, socially and professionally. I'm very thankful that it turned out the way it did, and I'm honored to be a part of it. It's the life I've always wanted. CSI

"Hodges has it in for me. Maybe one day we'll duke it out... I'm sure Bobby w

win hands down!" >>>>>>>>>>>>>>>>>> SEASON >

8

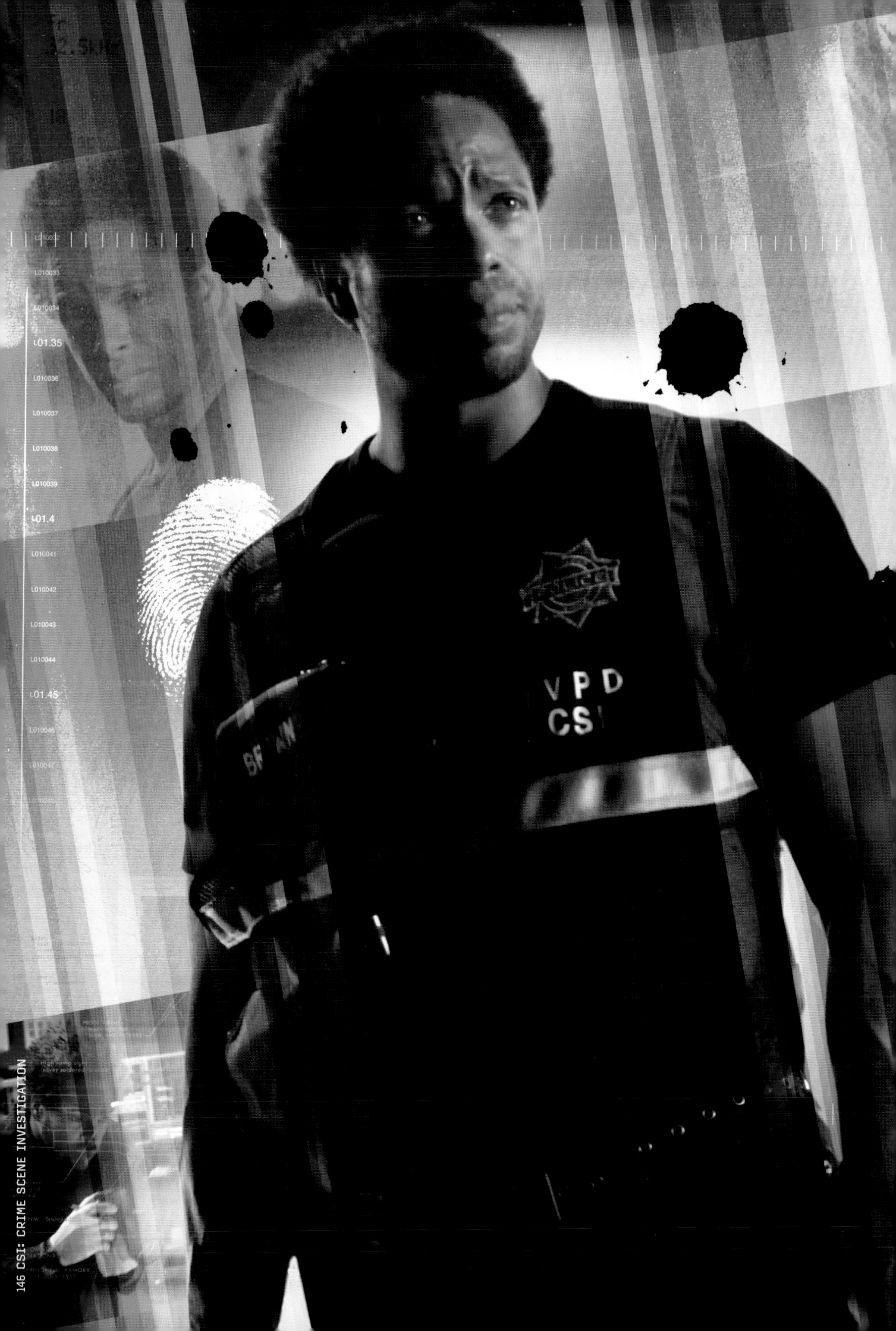
VPD
CSI

AS THE ONLY MEMBER OF GRISSOM'S TEAM BORN AND RAISED IN LAS VEGAS, WARRICK BROWN IS WELL AWARE OF THE CITY OF SIN'S SEDUCTIVE CHARMS. ACTOR GARY DOURDAN CHATS ABOUT THE INNER DEMONS THAT CONTINUE TO PLAGUE CSI: CRIME SCENE INVESTIGATION'S SMOOTHEST OPERATOR.

AGAINST THE ODDS

Warrick Brown's career as a CSI got off to a rocky start. While processing a crime scene, he abandoned rookie investigator Holly Gribbs without back-up so he could place a bet for a crooked judge. That decision cost her dearly when the felon came back and shot her. However, rather than dismiss him, Grissom gave Warrick a second chance, although there have been plenty of other hard knocks for him over the years. It was those flaws and rough edges that made Warrick more three dimensional than most cookie cutter cops which was what ultimately piqued actor Gary Dourdan's interest in the CSI series.

"I was really smitten with the character," recalls Dourdan in an exclusive interview. "I hadn't read anything that strong from any other pilot. Anthony Zuiker wrote this character with a lot of strong attitude and dialogue. I was actually very surprised it stuck and stayed on screen. Jerry Bruckheimer backed him up and Billy [Petersen] was right there. He called me after the audition and said, 'Man, I am really happy to work with you.' I was so naïve and didn't even really know anything about the project. It was all happening so fast. I was like, 'So are you one of the producers?' and he was like, 'Yeah, and I am also in it. I am playing Grissom.' I was thinking 'Oh my God! I loved you in To Live And Die In L.A.!' He was my hero. That movie changed my whole perception of film. I was a big fan and they just grabbed me up."

Despite diverse credits ranging from A Different World and Alien: Resurrection to Impostor and Soul Food, Dourdan's rising star status hardly ensured him a place on the CSI: Crime Scene Investigation cast.

"I went into that audition and there were 10 very well known black actors that were walking from room to room for that role for about four days," explains Dourdan. "They whittled it down to four and then even more. I just kept on going in and giving the same read as I saw the character. Anthony, Jerry, and Billy gave me a lot of support and it charged the hell out of me. You just try and be cool with all the praise coming at you because this business can be very fickle. I was very reserved but I am very proud they opened that door for me."

Sexy and somber, online profiles list Warrick as an audio/visual expert, yet it is his intuitive nature, commitment, vast connections, and colorful history that have distinguished him from his colleagues.

"Besides the obvious, Warrick was born and raised in Las Vegas," says Dourdan. "Attached to that is the way he looks at a crime scene and he's a detective so he knows human language, how people lie, what people are up to, and the patterns of crime. He understands people of the street, he's gambled, so he knows that whole game. It is not just

> ## "I would certainly like Catherine and Warrick's relationship to evolve and the audience to see something that is natural happen."

straight science for him, even though we try to process as much as we can to be able to prove beyond a shadow of a doubt whether a person is guilty or, on occasion, innocent."

Furthermore, personal details such as Warrick's obsessive gambling, drug usage, and maverick attitude have often marked him as the bad boy of the team. "When I first read some of it, I had a problem with that," notes Dourdan. "I was almost developing a complex because the character gets into trouble all the time. Then it was fun to play the drama and those idiosyncrasies. Negative or positive, that is what makes my work interesting. It is boring to play the good guy all the time; it gets pretty bland.

"There have been some episodes where we've struggled to grab more out of his vices than, 'You gamble, you lose money, you are a sad guy,'" adds Dourdan. "You have seen that a thousand times so let's go some places where there is no way out. Let's have some serious conflicts and maybe some resolution at the end. A lot of people believe once a gambler, always a gambler."

MUSIC MAESTRO

To unwind and blow off steam, Warrick DJs at a friend's club and even writes some of his own

material. Ironically, that facet is art imitating life since Dourdan is a multi-instrumentalist in real life with an extreme passion for music.

"That wasn't my idea," notes Dourdan. "I was opposed to it but Danny Cannon kept pushing it. We found somewhere in the middle that Warrick had this underground jazz vibe going on. That was something that appealed to me more because there was a possibility that could happen. And we are in Las Vegas. I used to live in New York and had five jobs. I was working at a bar, security, another theater, and I was a chef, so you do what you can to survive. Being a crime scene investigator is a career but I can see Warrick being a pianist in a jazz bar in order to make ends meet. Getting into law enforcement was his way of getting some security in his life, so the music wasn't my idea but I went along with it."

Established in the pilot was a healthy competition between Warrick and LVPD team mate Nick Stokes. Not only are the two frequently paired up on cases but they enjoy teasing and pressing each other's buttons. That kind of chemistry can't be easily faked and it should be no surprise to anyone that Dourdan and co-star George Eads are very good pals off screen as well.

WHO ARE YOU?

WARRICK BROWN PROFILE

It was perhaps inevitable Warrick Brown would fall prey to Las Vegas' main source of income and become a gambling addict – he's the one member of the CSI team who was born and bred in "The Entertainment Capital Of The World." In the pilot (1.01), Warrick's compulsion contributed to the death of rookie CSI Holly Gribbs; Grissom chose to reprimand rather than fire him and lose another CSI. Raised by his grandmother after the death of his mother when he was seven, Warrick doesn't know his father but has strong relations with Grissom and fellow CSI Nick. He and Nick flipped a coin for the fake case that saw Nick entombed in the *Grave Danger* episodes (5.23 and 5.25) and Warrick's guilt at sending his friend to his fate was instrumental in his settling down. He married Tina at a drive-through chapel the day before *Bodies In Motion* (6.01) takes place – upsetting Catherine, with whom he'd shared a special moment while investigating the storm drains during *Down The Drain* (5.02). Nick refers to tough times in *Bang-Bang* (6.23) – "I hear your marriage is on the rocks…" – but it's not until *Leapin' Lizards* (7.22) that Warrick reveals it's over, wishing Tina had understood his job. He's unlikely to be short of female attention now he's single; when re-examining evidence in *Mea Culpa* (5.09), Warrick mentions having dated the assistant manager at the Flamingo casino and how he still gets, "free steak and eggs every Sunday morning", leading Nick to quip: "Free steak and eggs means she didn't know about the flight attendant…" And he can always woo women with music; when investigating the death of a singer's wife in *Grissom Versus The Volcano* (4.09), Warrick shows off his talent with a few bars on the piano in the dead woman's hotel suite.

WHIMSICAL WARRICK
Memorable Brown musings...

"I ain't getting down on my knees for nobody.
You can shoot me!" – *Pilot*

"Entomology is our friend."
– *Friends & Lovers*

"Laws don't end when you come to Vegas!"
– *To Halve And To Hold*

"I hate lawyers. I hate court.
They all need to dry up and die."
– *Viva Las Vegas*

"Hey pop. Like the Buddha said to the monk. Make me
one with everything." – *Viva Las Vegas*

L010036

TRIVIA

In 1994, Gary starred with Marg
Helgenberger in an unsuccessful
television pilot entitled *Keys*.

L010039

> ## "Not in my wildest dreams did I ever think Quentin Tarantino would come to TV and direct our show. That has got to be the wildest dream ever! Three shows before that, we were dragging our knuckles and he came on and beat the crap out of us."

"We have been real buddies since we started the show," says Dourdan. "We were hanging and crashing at each other's houses. George would come out to Venice and then I would go to his crib when mine was being renovated. Camaraderie is so important to the show. It is a good dynamic and ours is real and genuine. For our characters, it is a positive reinforcement for American society to see two cats working together that are from two different ends of the cultural spectrum and have a harmonious relationship with each other."

With such a close bond, Warrick was understandably upset when Nick was abducted and buried alive in the season five finale, *Grave Danger*. It proved to be one of

CSI's most intense hours but what further elevated the episode was the involvement of *Pulp Fiction*'s Quentin Tarantino.

"Not in my wildest dreams did I ever think Quentin would come to TV and direct our show," smiles Dourdan. "That has got to be the wildest dream ever! Three shows before that, we were dragging our knuckles on the ground and he came on and beat the crap out of us. There were so many cooks in the kitchen that we ended up making it into a two-parter. I have mixed feelings about the episode but it was fantastic to work with such a genius. Also, I pushed him and he pushed me. I was like, 'What this show is missing is a Quentinism, a Tarantino-esque royale with cheese!' Quentin was like, 'Alright, alright, alright! Give me a minute!' He goes into his trailer and comes back out two hours later with two and a half pages. I was like, 'What have I done? Why did I open my mouth?' I read it and was so excited."

And even though Nick was rescued from his bug-infested deathtrap, the whole traumatic ordeal

caused Warrick to re-evaluate his life. As a result, viewers were stunned to learn that over the show's summer hiatus, Warrick apparently tied the knot with Las Vegas nurse Tina.

"To be completely honest, that did come out of nowhere," confirms Dourdan about the development. "The season before, they were writing in that Warrick and Catherine had the makings of a romance or hitting it on the desk. She was throwing it at me and I was throwing it back. Of course, we weren't making it up on the spot; it was in the script. So a summer passed, I came back, and Warrick is married. It happened so abruptly and I questioned why, what is the valid reason? I was never given one. I can only speculate there were issues in a certain area or maybe that it was something that added drama to our dynamic because in a couple of episodes lately, our characters have been volleying back and forth a little bit again. I would certainly like the latter to evolve and the audience to see something that is natural happen."

TRIVIA
Gary is a talented musician. He plays the drums, guitar, piano, bass and sax.

PUSHING THE ENVELOPE

On top of the complex CSI characters, part of what makes the crime-solving drama so appealing are the bizarre murders and circumstances. Even the strongest stomachs gave a little heave when a liquefied decomposed body spilled out of a duffel bag in one episode, yet Dourdan feels the writers could push the envelope even further in some areas.

"We've had fights over whether we can say this or do that," offers Dourdan. "I've had artistic struggles with certain directors. We are always trying to compete with cable networks that have no leash at all. And competing with those shows on an artistic and critical level is very difficult. We seem to get away with the science and the horror of the forensic drama. I am always shocked when the knife goes into the body. I know it is movie magic

GARY DOURDAN'S SCREEN CREDITS

The pick of Gary's TV and film career to date...

Doorman (2008)
– as Dominick
Music comedy drama due for release before the end of the year.

Impostor (2001)
– as Captain Burke
Gary stars alongside *CSI: NY*'s Gary Sinise in this sci-fi thriller based on the gripping short story by acclaimed writer Philip K. Dick.

Alien: Resurrection (1997)
– as Christie
Fourth instalment of the hugely popular sci-fi franchise starring Sigourney Weaver. Gary takes fifth billing as Christie.

A Different World (1992)
– as Shazza Zulu
Gary appeared in 13 episodes of this long-running and popular comedy series.

TRIVIA
Gary has two children – a daughter, Nyla, and a son, Lyric.

but I wince and my toes curl up. I watch it the same as anyone else and when we are doing the show, we don't know the effects they are putting on things. It often morphs into something different, so I am surprised we get away with a lot of that. I fight constantly because they are not comfortable with showing a certain sexuality and I think we can get away with more. But that is part of the job and we try to be collaborative."

In retrospect, Warrick has been pretty lucky. Sara has been kidnapped, Nick trapped alive, Greg beaten up badly, and Catherine drugged and abused but somehow he has escaped relatively unscathed so far.

"Early, early, early on, Warrick was under the thumb of a hardcore judge," reminds Dourdan. "The judge used Warrick for his own bidding. That was a heavy situation to be in. Then, of course, Warrick creates his own drama with his gambling. Other than that, you are right. Remember in the pilot he was a little too blasé about the newbie and got her killed. That is something I would like Warrick to carry with him everyday. His trouble has been more internal rather than being in a bad situation where someone has grabbed him like Sara Sidle or Nick Stokes. Being as large as he is doesn't hurt either."

With interests in martial arts, and music, not to mention a growing résumé of television, theater, and movie roles, it seems Dourdan has done it all, yet the down-to-earth Philadelphia native feels the best is yet to come.

"Oh man! I haven't even scratched the surface!" he concludes. "You ain't seen anything yet! I would like to work on music videos and I would certainly like to direct this film my brother wrote that we started shooting in Rome. We started breaking ground on that. I am really getting closer to getting the music into movies or musicals. I have been having a great time over the years recording a lot of different acts. I have worked with Run DMC for the Live 8 event, recorded a remake of a Jimi Hendrix song with him, and put some poetry in there. It is just involving myself in the things that are going on right now too, like helping the people in New Orleans, or the guys coming back home after being smacked around in the desert. They have no pensions now. It is also about creating a union with the world, and one way is through music which is universal." CSI

THE ENEMY WITHIN

For four seasons CONOR O'FARRELL was the dependable, if standoffish, Undersheriff Jeffrey McKeen. And then came the *For Gedda/For Warrick* two-parter. The detective everyone now loves to hate talks about his time on the show, secrecy, and fan reactions...

Conor O'Farrell clearly relishes his status as one of US TV's most in-demand character actors. For someone who never considered acting before college ("I was mainly an athlete when I was young"), a workshop led to a quickly developed taste for the thespian lifestyle. After years in the theater, O'Farrell decided to move back home to his LA roots and try his hand at TV and movies, mostly, as he admits, because it meant a little more job security than the nomadic stage world. "I felt like there was going to have to be a time if I was to make a career out of this, that I was going to have to come back out here and work in film and TV. There's more stability to it, financially you can support a family with it, and so it worked out well for me."

It certainly has – he's appeared on everything from *NYPD Blue* to the late, lamented *Dark Skies*. Yet he'd all but given up on trying to land parts in *CSI* when his luck changed. "It was funny," he says. "I auditioned for *CSI* when it was shooting up in Santa Clarita. I went in half a dozen times for different roles and Carol Kritzer, the casting director, is an old friend of mine, and almost every time I felt I did okay but I didn't get the job. After a while, I talked to my agent and said, 'I've been in there several times, they know what I do. I really don't want to drive in and audition again, because I'm not giving them what they want.' And then they had this role, in the Quentin Tarantino

episode, *Grave Danger*, and they'd already cast, the sheriff of Las Vegas. But he wasn't available for some reason, so they decided to introduce this character, the undersheriff. It was just supposed to be for that one episode, I think. My agent told me they were just going to give it to me, and I didn't have to read."

Originally planned as a one-shot deal, O'Farrell's role as Jeffrey McKeen soon turned into a recurring role he could squeeze in around other work. "We really never had a discussion about it being recurring. I would get a call every so often that they wanted me for another *CSI* and I'd go and look at it. Obviously you'd have discussions with the director about the scenes, but there never really was a decision about McKeen's past. I didn't know how long I was going to be on it. I treated every episode like this could be my last one. And it kept going, which was great. We had more discussion about the last two – for obvious reasons!"

At the end of season eight and the beginning of season nine, McKeen's role shifted from dogged cop to scheming killer. "It was funny because in the previous episodes there was no indication that I was anything but a bureaucrat. There was nothing to suggest I was involved in any sort of graft. And all of a sudden I had this past that I didn't know I had!" And he also had no idea that he'd be gunning down Gary Dourdan's Warrick Brown in the episode

For Gedda until just before it happened... "When it came to the night before we were shooting the final scene, one of the producers came up to me with an envelope, because that scene was omitted from the scripts. It was like the CIA: 'This is an envelope. This is the final scene. It's for you, a couple of other people, and that's it. Don't talk to anyone about it!'"

And what about the fan reaction to the undersheriff's murderous turn? It makes him laugh. "I went on the *CSI* blog site. And the way people were chatting about the character! 'I knew that son of a bitch was a bad guy! He's going to go to prison and be someone's prison bitch!'" he chuckles. "I was going, 'Holy cow... These people are taking this seriously!' I was amazed at the reaction."

With McKeen safely behind bars – and probably very good friends with a large man named Bunny – O'Farrell thinks his time on the show is likely now at an end. He's not worried, though – he has some theater work lined up and 2010 will see the debut of one of his more recent jobs. "I'm in an HBO miniseries, the sequel to *Band Of Brothers*, called *The Pacific*. That's a big job. It's turning into the biggest production in TV history. It's a big deal – Steven Spielberg and Tom Hanks are producing again." World War Two? It's a good thing he's got an itchy trigger finger... CSI

"All of a sudden I had this past that I didn't know I had!" >>>>>>>>>>>>>

SEASON 9

WARRICK BROWN'S **BRUTAL SHOOTING**
IN *FOR GEDDA* STUNNED *CSI* FANS ALL
OVER THE WORLD, AND THE AFTERSHOCKS
ARE STILL BEING FELT. WITH HIS VEGAS
COLLEAGUES STILL IN MOURNING IN THE
OPENING EPISODES OF SEASON NINE,
WE PAY TRIBUTE TO THIS UNFORGETTABLE
CHARACTER BY PRESENTING HIS DEFINING
MOMENTS...

A LUCKY BREAK

Warrick almost loses his job

When? *Pilot/Cool Change*, season 1, pilot/episode 2

What? A natural born gambler, Warrick strikes it lucky when Grissom allows him to stay on the team despite deserving to lose his job. His gambling addiction proved too strong in the pilot episode, causing him to break protocol and leave a new CSI at a crime scene alone. Little did he know that his personal misdemeanor would lead to Holly Gribbs getting shot, and dying. Warrick took her death hard... and personally.

"I went to lay a bet. I didn't even think I was doing anything wrong."

ARRICK

TOUGH AT THE TOP

Grissom puts Warrick in charge of the nightshift

When? Ellie, season two, episode 10

What? Warrick's given another show of faith by Grissom when he's put in charge of the nightshift. It's a busy night, as always, but not only does Warrick have the pressures of the cases to deal with (and with one of them involving Captain Brass' daughter it's not an easy task!), he also has to manage the team – his usual co-workers. As a good friend, Nick is supportive, but Sara takes every opportunity to challenge him. Warrick manages to keep his cool, and asserts his authority with the right balance of power and diplomacy, proving that he is worthy of the responsibility Grissom gave him.

"It's my case. Tonight I'm the primary... If you have a problem with that you can clock out now. Am I clear?"

THE HEART OF THE MATTER

Warrick gets emotionally involved in a case

When? Random Acts Of Violence, season three, episode 13

What? Warrick's heart leads his head when friends from his childhood are involved in a case, and his old coach's daughter is killed. Convinced that a former school troublemaker is responsible, Warrick makes it his personal mission to bring him to justice. Unfortunately for everybody concerned, his lack of objectivity clouds his judgment. Even after Grissom takes him off the case, Warrick can't distance himself. His misplaced persistence leads to widespread repercussions, and another bout of personal guilt, again having to admit to Grissom that he "blew it."

"I'm not a robot okay? I actually care about these people."

ROWN 1970 2008

SMOOTH OPERATOR

We see Warrick enjoying life outside work

When? *Grissom Versus The Volcano*, season four, episode nine / *Mea Culpa*, season five, episode nine

What? Luckily, life as a CSI isn't all doom and gloom! And if you happen to be as charming and talented (not to mention good looking!) as Mr. Brown, then you'll certainly have plenty going on to take your mind off work. At one point he was seeing an assistant hotel manager who was so keen on him, she continued to give him special treatment after they broke up – free ham and eggs every Sunday! Perhaps he wooed her with a romantic tune on the piano? He certainly has the skills (as we see briefly in *Grissom Versus The Volcano*). To quote Warrick on another guy who seemingly has it all…

"This guy's got it made."

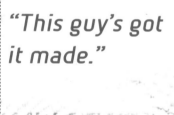

BRIEF ENCOUNTER

Warrick and Catherine share a moment

When? *Down The Drain*, season five, episode two

What? Warrick and Catherine find themselves in an unusual situation – wading through flooded underground drains. Upon surfacing, Catherine falls and Warrick catches her in his arms. They stare at each other for several seconds, neither wanting to let go. There is an obvious spark between them, and we're intrigued to know what they're going to do next. But the moment is short-lived, as they're interrupted. Damn!

"You alright?"

HEADS YOU WIN, TAILS YOU LOSE

Warrick feels guilty and helpless when Nick is buried alive

When? *Grave Danger*, season five, episodes 24 & 25

What? Warrick wrestles with his emotions when the team fight to save Nick. As a close friend of the buried CSI, Warrick struggles to stay calm and can't forget the fact that he and Nick flipped a coin for the case – it could just as easily have been him in that torturous situation. He watches the video feed of Nick pulling a gun and can't put the image out of his head. His anxiety eventually reaches boiling point and he lashes out at Greg. However, after a few typical Quentin Tarantino plot twists, Warrick is there to rescue his buddy, even lifting the coffin lid and riding to the hospital with Nick.

"I just can't help but think that it could have been me in that box, you know? We flipped a coin for that… I wouldn't have lasted for this long."

THAT'S WHAT FRIENDS ARE FOR

Warrick expresses concern about his marriage

When? *Leapin' Lizards*, season seven, episode 22

What? Warrick's friendship with fellow CSI Nick is a prime example of how close the CSI team can be. Though they have a professional rivalry, out of work they enjoy a beer or two together, and these guys are comfortable enough to share their feelings and support each other. As we saw at the end of season five, Nick's brush with death shook Warrick. Possibly as a reaction to this, Warrick suddenly married his girlfriend, Tina. Sadly, this hasty union proved problematic. Warrick airs his concerns with Nick, and, like any good friend, Nick gives his advice with a touch of humor. The pair even jokingly call each other "baby" and "honey!"

"I don't know, man, maybe it would work out better if Tina was someone who did what we did. At least she'd understand the hours."

TROUBLE AND STRIFE

Warrick's troubled personal life interferes with his work

When? *Cockroaches*, season eight, episode nine

What? Warrick arrives late to a crime scene after an argument over divorce proceedings and appears exhausted and agitated. We learn that he is now reliant on prescription drugs. Things go from bad to worse as he continues his shift in an unstable manner, and, as we've seen before, attempts to take matters into his own hands. But with the case involving Lou Gedda, a Mob boss and strip-club owner, this is far from a wise idea! Visiting Gedda's strip-joint, Warrick orders champagne with no intention of paying for it, in the hope of getting a beat down so he can bust the bad guys. When this fails he follows one of the lap dancers to another bar to grill her about Gedda, and in his confused state, goes home with her. But this seriously backfires when the stripper is found dead in his car!

"This whole divorce is taking the wind out of my sails... I feel kind of disconnected."

UNDER THE SPOTLIGHT

Warrick is questioned over his involvement with the lap dancer and her death

When? *Lying Down With Dogs*, season eight, episode 10

What? Despite the concoction of drugs and alcohol consumed the night of the lap dancer's murder, Warrick is convinced he remembers the events as they happened, and that he is not responsible. After harsh questioning, he is let off without being charged. Of course, Warrick being Warrick does not leave it there. After fingerprints of a local tramp are found in his car, he believes more than ever that Lou Gedda is behind the death, and that he framed the tramp. He presents this theory to Grissom, saying he wants to work the case. Of course, Grissom tells Warrick to distance himself. When the accused tramp won't name Gedda or his men, Warrick bursts in on the interview. Exhausted of warnings, Grissom suspends Warrick instantly.

"I didn't kill her but I know damn well who did."

 IN TOO DEEP

Warrick is framed for Lou Gedda's murder and then shot

When? *For Gedda*, season eight, episode 17

What? Warrick's back at work, but when a private investigator turns up dead, it transpires that he was hired by Warrick to prove Gedda's guilt. Warrick, still obviously suffering from stress, receives a phone call to go to Gedda's club. Unable to see the wood for the trees, he goes, and the next thing he knows, he's been framed for Gedda's murder. Luckily, with help from his team, Warrick's innocence is proved and corruption elsewhere in the force is exposed. The team celebrate over breakfast, but as Warrick gets into his car to drive home, he is stopped by the Undersheriff who asks whether he plans to root out the mole within the LVPD. When Warrick replies to the affirmative, the Undersheriff shoots him.

"As far as I'm concerned, there's no place I'd rather be."

RIME
LAUREN
LEE
SMITH

MEET THE NEWEST MEMBER OF GRISSOM'S TEAM... RILEY ADAMS.

Throughout her career, Lauren Lee Smith certainly hasn't played it safe. Long before *CSI*, the Canadian actress was decked out in black leather as the telepath Emma on *Mutant X*, then embraced her inner lesbian for *The L Word*, starred in the sexually risqué *Lie With Me*, demonstrated a dark side in the recent feature film *Pathology*, and is currently awaiting the release of the horror anthology *Trick 'r Treat*. Based on this evidence, it should be no surprise to anyone that Smith's latest gig as rookie Riley Adams on *CSI: Crime Scene Investigation* is yet another intriguing polar opposite to her previous projects.

"This is something I've never done before," explains the extremely upbeat Smith. "The last few years, I've worked on a lot of independent films, so I was pleasantly

surprised a network television show wanted to have me in the first place. It was just really exciting to come onto a well established show, be a part of something so well loved, and to step into a whole new world that I haven't had the opportunity to experience until now. *The L Word* was on Showtime and a bit edgier, so it's not quite the same, and, with *Mutant X*, I just felt like I was such a baby. That was my first real job, so it was sort of just a flash."

With names such as *Battlestar Galactica*'s Katee Sackhoff rumored to have been vying for the coveted role of Riley Adams, surely the audition for one of television's top-rated series was an arduous affair?

"This is going to sound really horrible, but it wasn't at all," says Smith. "There is a long and short answer. I did a pilot for CBS in April, and that was an experience in itself. I had to jump through a thousand hoops as far as network testing goes. That was difficult and it didn't get picked up. Then the day it didn't, I heard they were interested in me for the new character on *CSI*. It just happened and I kind of feel guilty. I did sit down with the showrunners, producers, and writers, because they hadn't seen me in person. They had only seen my demo reel and the recent work I had done, so we had a meet and greet to see if we all meshed."

Obviously, Smith impressed the heck out of them, but they weren't about to make her *CSI* introduction an easy one. In fact, Riley joins the team under some tough circumstances due to Sara's sudden departure and Warrick's tragic murder in season eight.

"When Riley arrives, she doesn't really know what the hell is going on," reveals Smith. "Riley has been brought to Vegas (to be a part of this) team and she is crazy about her job. That's what she's there to do, so she doesn't really take much notice of the drama that is surrounding the CSIs right now. When we first meet Riley, she tells it like it is. She has a wicked sense of humor, is kind of a smart ass, and sassy. She throws people off guard by being so abrupt with the other CSIs, who don't know what to expect. We are playing with this idea that she tells one person some of her background and then turns around to spin a completely different tale to someone else. No one really has a sense of who exactly this girl is or where she comes from right now."

U nderstandably, the remaining crime investigators are still grieving and in no mood to embrace any new blood. "They are a little wary of this girl, of who she is, and how capable she is," confirms Smith. "At the same time, they are understaffed so they do need her. Riley knows there is no time for formalities or chit-chat – it's just time to work. Gradually, we see Catherine coming around, but Riley has to prove herself."

In addition, Riley is arguably an odd choice considering she is the only CSI who has not been mentored by Grissom.

"It's interesting because we are beginning to see Riley and Grissom butt heads a little, but there is still a certain amount of respect. Riley is not afraid to speak her mind," reports Smith. "If she believes in something, she shows a lot of conviction for it and isn't willing to back down until she's proven wrong. Grissom understands that and respects it because Riley does it in a way that is somewhat humorous. It's an interesting dynamic and she does push his buttons a little to see how far she can take it."

Already, Riley has accompanied all of her teammates to various crime scenes, which means Smith has been exposed to some truly gory sights...

"I really dig all that. I find it fascinating," offers Smith. "The more bizarre the better. I got to do my ride-along and go to the crime lab – I eat all that up. I had been to the LA county morgue for the movie *Pathology* so I didn't have the pleasure of going back. All of that stuff is so fascinating and one of the reasons I love this job so much is that, as an actor, I am allowed to explore these strange worlds and find out all of this information. I love the gross stuff. I have lots of brothers!" (Laughs)

Smith's siblings couldn't prepare her for all the procedural lingo, though.

"Everything was going pretty smoothly for me, and then yesterday, it was like I drank a bowl of stupid," she laughs. "Eric (Szmanda) and I were

doing my first walk and talk and I felt so bad. It was a Steadicam shot, too – our operator was following us, and those cameras are heavy. It seemed like every time I got it right, Eric didn't, or if he got it, I messed it up. I think we did it 25 times, so it was pretty embarrassing. Other than that, it's been okay, as long as I give myself enough time to know exactly what it is I'm saying."

That tongue-twisting jargon isn't the only incident that could potentially sneak its way onto a blooper reel...

"The first day I was coming on to do my scene, I had butterflies in my stomach and the first assistant director was like, 'Everyone, this is Lauren. Lauren, meet everyone,'" recalls Smith. "I'm wearing heels and I totally wiped out! That was typical of me, though, because I am very clumsy. In the lab, there are all these glass doors and once a month, someone runs into it. I'm sure I am up soon."

F rom the sounds of it, one aspect Smith didn't need to fake was Riley's new kid at the lab jitters. After all, *CSI* is one of the most popular television series on the planet and her first primetime gig. "I was definitely apprehensive and

nervous," notes Smith. "I am a fan of *CSI*, as is my whole family and the rest of the world. I have to say I was immediately put at ease on a personal level by everybody. The entire cast is lovely. They are such a family at this point that they really welcomed me with open arms. It's been a really easy transition and such a pleasure to come to work."

Nonetheless, relocating to Los Angeles from her native Canada initially re-enforced those nerves.

"It was a bit of a culture shock, but I'm getting into it now," says Smith. "We had a hiatus for about a month, so I spent some time going, 'Okay, I'm living in LA now and that's different. I've got a dog. I could get used to this.' Previously, a lot of my work had been filmed in Canada. It's great because my family have lived in LA on and off since I was 14-years-old so I do have a few good family friends in the area. I talk to my mom and it's cold and pouring with rain in Vancouver. I'm like, 'Oh really? It's hot here and I'm going to the beach.'"

To date, Smith has only filmed a handful of episodes, but she is absolutely giddy over being on *CSI* and the direction they are heading with her character.

"I've really enjoyed the humorous moments that the writers put in and what we are allowed to bring to our own characters," offers Smith. "They are very open to our own ideas and little character quirks, so that has been great. As for the character's arc, butting heads with Grissom, and being the girl who is the opposite of cerebral coming in and instinctively letting her guts lead her, is interesting, but it can also get her in a lot of trouble."

With her role in *Pathology* and now *CSI*, it appears Smith was destined to mess around in the world of forensics.

"God, what's not to like?" enthuses Smith. "Forensics just fascinate me. I had no idea half of the technology that is available existed and what it is able to do. We have these wonderful technical advisors on set who are always open to us asking questions about how everything works. These are people who were actual CSIs and they talk about how much it's changed in a short time. It's insane how it's evolved, even in the last 10 years.

"And every single tiny aspect of it, what human beings are capable of, and the technology, is mind boggling," she continues. "To be quite honest, it's interesting that these people, especially the pathologists, can go in there and see these horrific things and not feel fazed at all. It's the same with the CSIs. They are able to look at it and say, 'Okay, these are horrible events and I can't change them, so the only thing I can do is figure out the how.' That whole mentality is fascinating. On a personal level, I couldn't do that at all." CSI

"*When we first meet Riley, she tells it like it is. She has a wicked sense of humor, is kind of a smart ass, and sassy!*"

↑ *"Quotation"*

When William Petersen announced he was leaving *CSI* to return to the stage, fans feared the worse. But CBS had an ace up its sleeve in the form of Hollywood A-lister LAURENCE FISHBURNE. In an exclusive interview, *The Matrix* star reveals why he and *CSI* were the perfect fit...

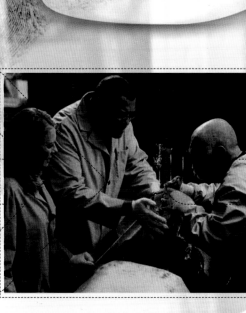

reloaded

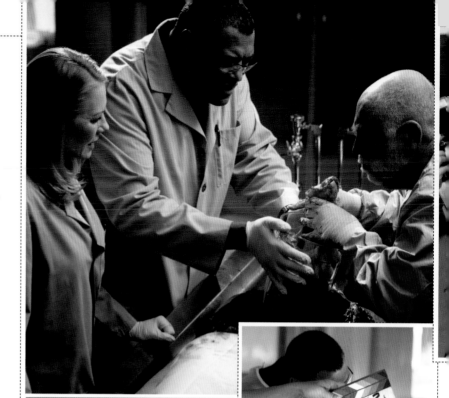

Somebody should bottle Laurence Fishburne's talent. The 47-year-old actor put the cool into *The Matrix* trilogy with his reality-altering turn as Morpheus, and captivated audiences in such films as *What's Love Got To Do With It*, *Mission: Impossible III*, *Boyz N The Hood* and *Akeelah And The Bee*. Although he's conquered the silver screen and stage (Fishburne is also a Tony Award winner), the Georgia native hasn't called television home since he wore a cowboy outfit in 1987's *Pee-wee's Playhouse*. Which is why it came as such a surprise when CBS announced that he would be playing Dr. Raymond Langston on *CSI: Crime Scene Investigation*.

"Really, the appeal was the material," says Fishburne in his familiar deep voice. "The writing on *CSI* is really first rate. After I had the chance to watch a couple of episodes and sit down with the producers, I felt really confident that we would be a good fit for each other."

In truth, the timing couldn't have been better. After nine seasons, William Petersen and his bug-loving Gil Grissom decided to move on to other endeavors. As a result of this changing of the guard, some critics claimed that the inaugural *CSI* series wouldn't survive without its leading man, and any chance it had would be down to Fishburne's A-list clout. It's a notion the actor fully rejects.

"They've been incredibly diligent in maintaining the level of storytelling and production values," counters Fishburne. "The attitude around here is that they are trying to do the best show possible and I think that is why *CSI* has such staying power. Everybody here really cares about the quality and it shows."

Indeed, it seems the creative staff took painstaking steps to ensure Langston wasn't a carbon copy of Grissom.

"I think we are two very different actors so I never concerned myself with any of that," notes Fishburne. "Grissom is beloved by all the viewers who enjoyed the show for all these years. And because of our differences I am kind of a welcome change, I hope."

Blood on his hands: (above) Langston gets to grips with the grim realities of his job.

To get a better handle on what their real-life counterparts go through, some of the *CSI* actors shadowed forensic investigators and did extra research. Fishburne, however, skipped that route.

"I didn't do anything in particular," he reports. "I've just been working with the writers and listening to their ideas. That's pretty much it. I have yet to do a forensic ride-along."

Introduced in *19 Down*, Langston was a medical doctor and pathologist whose former co-worker was an angel of death who killed 27 patients. Unable to see the evidence in front of his eyes, Langston wrote a book detailing the events, something Grissom read and liked. However, the two only meet after Grissom is forced to take a class that Langston is teaching, in the hope of determining the identity of a murderer.

"I was very happy with how Langston was established," reports Fishburne. "I liked the fact that he had Grissom's blessing. I thought that was very important for the audience that since he was leaving, Grissom should at least present a person who he deemed trustworthy and intelligent enough to be good at this job, or someone who had the desire to excel."

Impressed by his work ethic and determination, Grissom recruited Langston as a special consultant in *One To Go* (William Petersen's final episode) before eventually offering him an entry-level position at the Las Vegas crime lab.

"Everybody was really welcoming to me and excited I was coming," says Fishburne. "I was glad to be here. Billy has been here a long time and he was excited about me being here so it went really smoothly. There was no turbulence involved. I think all of the issues people might have were addressed with each character. Captain Brass, Catherine Willows, Nick Stokes, and everyone else had a different way of coping with Grissom's exit. All those things were done very well in the scripts and that came through in Billy's final episodes."

While the CSIs went out of their way to help Langston settle in and even invited him to a diner with them, a bitter Hodges did the exact opposite by giving him the cold shoulder. Obviously, Langston still had something to prove.

"It was great to have that kind of tension to play," agrees Fishburne. "Some obstacles are always good and are the cornerstone of drama."

I don't know it yet and hopefully it will reveal itself in further episodes. If anything, it totally strengthened his resolve."

Up until now, Fishburne has only cut his teeth in a handful of episodes and while some actors want to know the direction they are heading, Fishburne is just enjoying the ride.

"I don't really retain the stuff once I've done it," he says. "I'm approaching it as one long movie, so I'm going chapter by chapter and once the chapter is over, I'm done with it. I'm not really trying to find out what future episodes are about either. I'd rather just get a hold of the scripts, work with them, and try to make them as good as I can."

That doesn't mean Fishburne isn't hoping Langston's history won't be fleshed out.

"I'm sure it will be," he confirms. "I know they have some back story in mind but nothing I can talk about right now. Again, what's great about *CSI* is they manage to allow the audience to learn a little bit about each character over the years so it's not just procedural. They have a real good balance of murder mystery, forensics, and the characters. You're not only learning about the crime solving, you also come to know these investigators better each time out."

Television's long exhausting days have been known to wear people down, so how has it compared to the movie grind Fishburne has become accustomed to?

"It depends on who you talk to," he smiles. "Most people will tell you television is harder because of the hours. My experience is that this is very civilized and I'm enjoying it."

Certainly the transition was made even easier by *CSI*'s friendly environment and the dedicated cast involved.

"I love my job!" concludes Fishburne. "Marg [Helgenberger], George [Eads], and Wally [Langham] have all been great. I worked with Robert David Hall years ago so it's been nice reuniting with him again. Lauren Lee Smith and I are doing an episode now where the two of us are heavy in it and we are doing some amazing stuff. This is a really good crew." CSI

Out in the field for a breaking and entering, Langston definitely took a different approach to processing a crime scene than his teammates and even crossed the line when he interfered as a father smacked his son during an interrogation.

"Well, the main thing is it's such a new world for Langston, especially compared to the world he came from," offers Fishburne. "His curiosity is at a heightened level. He's much more inquisitive about everything he encounters on the job because he's so new.

"Langston is also a lot more interested in the people he encounters," he continues. "That's just human nature and the kind of person he is. Langston hasn't been around long enough to have built up an immunity. His sensitivity is something that may get the best of him."

In the opening sequence of *The Grave Shift*, Langston wastes plenty of brushes and powder attempting to lift some fingerprints. With a smile, a goodhearted Nick demonstrates the fine art of finesse. While Langston may be frustrated by his inexperience, Fishburne finds his character's rookie status far more interesting than if he had joined as a seasoned professional.

"It gives me a place to go," reasons Fishburne. "It's not like Langston has come in and said, 'I'm the new sheriff in town and this is how it's going to be!' Everything is a discovery so this is a wonderful thing to play as an actor."

At the end of that episode, Langston extended his hand to a troubled teenage boy, only to be spat in the face. That degrading act would have disillusioned even a veteran CSI, yet the newbie just seemed to take it all in stride.

"I think it was a complete shock to Langston," counters Fishburne. "If there is a lesson there,

▼ *"Quotation"*

"Langston hasn't been around long enough to have built up an immunity. His sensitivity is something that may get the best of him."

STARTER FOR 10

Into Season 10 Scrap Book

Family Affair: Sara – now Sara Sidle-Grissom – returns and offers her help while waiting to get more grant money for her and Gil's research, while the apparent drunk driver killing of a motorist becomes more complicated when it emerges that the driver was the victim's stalker.

Ghost Town: The CSI team investigate the murders of two unsavory characters, a porn producer and drug dealer, in a middle-class neighborhood.

Working Stiffs: The body of a handsome but cocky tech-geek at a casino is found bludgeoned to death in the woods, leading the team to a robbery plot gone bad.

Coup de Grace: A veteran cop who is advancing towards retirement shoots and kills a black man in a fast food joint and it looks as if the final shot was point blank, and after the man was already down on the ground. But is the racially charged incident what it looks like?

Death and the Maiden: What seems like a random beating in an alleyway, and a separate robbery/murder at a nearby electronics store, are actually two linked crimes.

Bloodsport: When a very popular local college football coach is found brutally murdered in his house, the team discover that one of the football players on the team has a terrible crime in his past which set the stage for the coach's murder.

From New York to Vegas: The CSIs investigate a murder at a bowling alley after a critical piece of evidence is revealed during a bowling tournament.

CSI: GL

THOSE ESSENTIAL CSI TERMS EXPLAINED IN HANDY A-Z FORMAT...

SCENE DO NOT CROSS   CRIME SCENE DO NOT CROSS   CRIME SCENE DO NOT CROSS   CRIME SC

PHONETIC ALPHABET

When spelling names, number plates, or addresses it is very important that similar sounding letters are not mixed up, so the phonetic alphabet is used by law enforcement officials in Las Vegas. For example CSI becomes 'Charlie, Sam, Ida'...

A – Adam	N – Nora
B – Baker	O – Ocean
C – Charlie	P – Paul
D – David	Q – Queen
E – Easy	R – Robert
F – Frank	S – Sam
G – George	T – Tom
H – Henry	U – Union
I – Ida	V – Victor
J – John	W – William
K – King	X – X-ray
L – Lincoln	Y – Yellow
M – Mary	Z – Zebra

ADIPOCERE
The soapy substance that occurs when bodies buried in moist gravesites decompose. Sometimes referred to by the unofficial name of "grave wax."

ANTHROPOLOGY
The science of human development and origins, which is applied to skeletal remains during an investigation.

ASPHYXIA
Occurs when a body is deprived of oxygen.

AUTOPSY
The examination of a dead body and its internal organs in order to determine cause of death.

BALLISTICS
Technically, ballistics is the study of a projectile in motion. Effectively, it is the science of firearm examination which attempts to match fired bullets and cartridge cases to each other and to suspected firearms. (See also Striation)

BLUNT FORCE TRAUMA (B.F.T.)
This physical injury is inflicted on a victim without breaking the skin surface, but can still cause internal injuries.

BLOOD SPATTER/ BLOODSTAIN INTERPRETATION
The examination of patterns of bloodstains to determine their nature and interrelationships in order to gain knowledge of the events surrounding a crime. The ultimate goal is to reconstruct a crime.

CALIBER
The approximate diameter of the inside of the bore of a firearm expressed in inches or millimeters.

CAST-OFF BLOOD
Blood that has traveled from the original source, such as a bleeding person or a dripping weapon.

CAUSE OF DEATH (C.O.D.)
The determination by the medical examiner of what fatal injury or disease "caused death."

DEOXYRIBONUCLEIC ACID (D.N.A.)
The genetic material that makes up all organic life. Every living thing has a unique DNA profile, which can be identified from bodily fluids or evidence such as hair, teeth, or bones. DNA is often used to match criminals to crimes.

ENTOMOLOGY
The study of insects and their development in different conditions, such as inside a decomposing body. Insects that are specifically associated with decomposing bodies are called carrion insects.

GAS CHROMATO- GRAPH (G.C.)
The use of a mobile phase, gas, passing over a stationary phase comprised of various solids, typically contained in a glass column to separate components in a mixture for identification.

GUNSHOT RESIDUE (G.S.R.)
The chemical residues left after a firearm is discharged. They are the remains of burned and unburned gunpowder as well as the chemicals from the priming compounds. Their presence and analysis can reveal the distance at which a firearm was discharged as well as the person that fired a firearm.

LATENT PRINT
The oils, amino acids and salts left when friction ridge skin contacts a surface. It is usually hidden from the naked eye and requires certain visualization methods such as black powder to develop them.

CRIME SCENE DO NOT CROSS   CRIME SCENE DO NOT CROSS   CRIME SC

LIVIDITY

The discoloration of the body by the gravitation of blood to the lower parts of the body after circulation stops. This can help determine time since death and movement of the body after death.

LUMINOL

A chemiluminescent compound used to detect cleaned-up bloodstains.

M.O.

Stands for "Method of Operation" and comes from the Latin, *Modus Operandi*.

NARCOTIC

An analgesic or painkilling substance that depresses vital body functions such as blood pressure, pulse rate, and breathing rate. The term "narcotics" has been used to describe almost all illegal drugs.

NINHYDRIN

A chemical used to detect fingerprints on porous materials such as paper.

ORTHOTOLIDINE SOLUTION

A chemical used to determine if a stain contains blood.

PATENT PRINT

A fingerprint that is visible. These are usually left behind in substances such as ink, paint, or blood.

PLASTIC PRINT

A visible fingerprint left behind in a malleable substance such as soap or wax.

POST MORTEM INTERVAL (P.M.I.)

The amount of time that has passed since a victim's death.

PUNCTURE WOUND

A wound that is not caused by a projectile, but a piercing wound usually made by a handheld object.

RAPE KIT

Items compiled by a criminal that facilitate commission of the crime of rape. Items such as duct tape or rope for restraint, condoms, gloves, etc. It is sometimes incorrectly used to refer to a sexual assault evidence collection kit used by investigators to collect evidence from a victim.

STRIATION

The distinct marking left on a bullet when it passes through the barrel of a gun.

TOXICOLOGY

The study of poisons and drugs and their effect on human and animal populations.

TRACE

Evidence deposited at a crime scene that is only discovered by a forensic investigation. This evidence is usually hair and fibers.

WHEN YOUR NUMBER'S UP

Police use short numerical codes to refer to crimes. They can vary from place to place, but here is a shortened list of the actual codes used by the LVPD...

401 – Accident (traffic)	416 – Fight
401A – Hit and run	417 – Family disturbance
402A – Arson	419 – Dead body
403 – Prowler	419A – Drowned person
405 – Suicide	420 – Homicide
406 – Burglary	420A – Murder/non-negligent homicide
409 – Drunk driver	
411 – Stolen motor vehicle	420B – Manslaughter
413 – Person with a gun	420Z – Attempted homicide
413A – Person with a knife	422 – Sick or injured officer
414 – Grand larceny	424 – Riot
415 – Assault	425 – Suspicious circumstances
415A – Assault with a gun	425A – Suspicious person(s)
415B – Assault with cutting device	425B – Suspicious vehicle
	426 – Rape
	426Z – Attempted rape
	427 – Kidnap
	428 – Child molest
	429 – Indecent exposure
	430 – Animal bite
	432 – Fraud
	433 – Stolen property
	434 – Illegal shooting
	435 – Embezzlement
	438 – Traffic citation
	440 – Wanted subject
	441 – Vandalism
	442 – Airplane crash
	444 – Officer needs help
	445 – Bomb threat

BLOOD SPECIMEN

BLOOD SPECIMEN

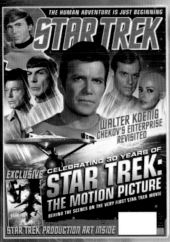

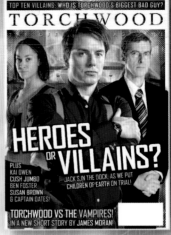